Professor ANDIAPPAN
2005

More Praise for *The Conflict Resolution Toolbox*

"We all know one thing about conflict: It is messy! Furlong's models offer mediators, facilitators, lawyers, psychotherapists and others 'a leg up' in more swiftly figuring out what is going on and what is needed. Furlong does not offer up a single 'truth,' style or theory, so much as a collection of effective tools that professionals, groups and families can use to better understand what they are experiencing and how they can approach achieving better results. Highly recommended."

James C. Melamed, J.D., CEO, Mediate.com

"A craftsperson is only as good as the tools they use. In this important new book, Gary Furlong provides the essential conflict resolution toolkit, offering a practical selection of specialized tools that will be useful to all conflict resolution craftspeople—novice and veteran alike."

Richard J. Weiler, LL.B., Chartered Mediator,
Fellow, International Academy of Mediators

"Gary has a remarkable ability to help fellow practitioners and clients alike achieve breakthroughs one wouldn't think possible. Anyone interested in constructively challenging their own thinking will find this toolbox practical and invaluable. His unique insights and strategies are powerful and truly distinguish him as a leading practitioner."

Leah Borsa, National Alternative Dispute Resolution Advisor, Parks Canada Agency

"In this well-written book, Gary Furlong provides eight practical and highly original models for analyzing and resolving conflict. Furlong's ingenious transformation of several important theories from psychology, sociology and other fields into models and worksheets, plus his illustration of how these models can be used with some highly emotional interpersonal clashes, give managers fresh ways to think about resolving common workplace conflicts. There is a model to fit various individual conflict resolution preferences and various types of quarrels. Don't miss this important new book—a must have for every manager's reference library!"

Dr. Carol A. Beatty, Director, Industrial Relations Centre;
Associate Professor, School of Business, Queen's University

"This incisive book will help mediators and others working with human conflicts experience the way that different lenses reveal vastly different views. This book will help our teaching, practicing, and thinking, and ultimately assist us in the complex and essential work of seeing things through multiple lenses."

Michelle LeBaron, Professor of Law and Director, UBC Program on Dispute Resolution

"This book's strength is in taking some central conflict resolution ideas from others and organizing them into a system of analysis in one handy source. The way analytical tools are presented, their practical usefulness and the depth at which Gary reviews them is new and helpful for practitioners, giving them a jumpstart in learning and growing."

Gordon Sloan, Partner, ADR Education, Victoria, BC

THE CONFLICT
RESOLUTION
TOOLBOX

THE CONFLICT
RESOLUTION
TOOLBOX

Models & Maps for Analyzing
Diagnosing
and Resolving Conflict

GARY T. FURLONG

John Wiley & Sons Canada, Ltd.

National Library of Canada Cataloguing in Publication Data

Furlong, Gary T.
    The conflict resolution toolbox : models & maps for analyzing, diagnosing, and resolving conflict / Gary Furlong.

Includes index.
ISBN-13 978-0-470-83517-6
ISBN-10 0-470-83517-6

1. Conflict management.   2. Mediation.   I. Title.
HM1126.F87 2005   303.6'9   C2005-900319-7

Production Credits:
Cover design: Mike Chan & Ian Koo
Interior text design: Adrian So R.G.D.
Front and back cover photo: Mike Chan
Printer: Tri-graphic Printing Ltd.

John Wiley & Sons Canada, Ltd
6045 Freemont Blvd.
Mississauga, Ontario
L5R 4J3

Printed in Canada
10 9 8 7 6 5 4 3 2 1

CONTENTS

FOREWORD

Several years ago my life-companion Susan and I decided to take a hiking vacation in France. We planned to walk a portion of the *Sentier de Grande Randonnée* (GR), a network of paths which, during the Middle Ages, were pilgrimage routes between towns and cities in the North of Europe and famous religious shrines in Southern France and Spain. While we were not on a religious pilgrimage per se, we did want to spend some good time together, be in touch with nature, and have a bit of tranquility (which we do not always find in our work as mediators). We also wanted to experience good French meals, village hospitality, and scenic walks through charming French countryside without losing our way, which we knew from past hikes in unknown territory was all too easy to do.

So, in preparation for our vacation, we acquired a number of maps—road maps, topographical maps, maps of towns and villages, maps that showed the way to noteworthy scenery, inns or restaurants. While it sounds like we are map fanatics, this is really not the case. We merely wanted to use them as tools to plan an exciting route along often poorly marked paths, across fields and streams and ultimately to the peace and quiet of local villages and inns (which we discovered were often few and far between). Once we had planned a general route, and could use the maps to pick out landmarks to locate ourselves as we proceeded, we were able to improvise, take side trips, stop at interesting spots, and find routes around any unexpected barriers that we encountered. Maps are wonderful tools. Oh that we had them for many other aspects of our lives!

While two people traversing an unknown rural landscape is not the same as navigating one's way through a conflict, it is remarkable how similar the two are. In both situations, the people involved have to locate themselves at any given point in time (geographically or relationally), identify significant "signposts" that indicate direction (progress, backtracking, wrong turns or detours), and develop successful strategies to handle a wide variety of unforeseen circumstances such as the washed out physical or emotional "bridge" needed to cross a barrier, overcome vicious dogs and strong feelings, and find needed resting places. Successful navigation when hiking is greatly facilitated by having a map, however, maps that help people navigate difficulties in relationships and other life conflicts are often few and far between.

Gary Furlong's new work, *The Conflict Resolution Toolbox*, is a valuable compilation and explication of "maps" that can be used by professional conflict management practitioners and others involved in disputes, to better handle and resolve differences. Drawing on the work of a number of conflict theorists and practitioners, he presents a range of models and maps, which anyone involved in conflict, will find useful in. He has developed a range of possible productive approaches and strategies to regulate destructiveness, manage disagreements, resolve differences, and positively transform conflicted relationships. Gary is careful to note that no one map can provide a sure and successful route through every conflict, but his collection is sure to provide multiple sources of insight and assistance in the development of a number of plausible trails to resolution.

In the work, Gary provides a detailed overview of a number of models and maps, demonstrates how they can be applied to specific cases and points the way for conflict analysts and strategists to become reflective practitioners—people who can understand and creatively respond to and resolve disputes when they are in them, and reflective learners who can gain insights from analysis of past experiences.

The Conflict Resolution Toolbox should be one of the essential works on the bookshelf, (and better yet in the briefcase) of any person who wants to gain a greater understanding of the causes, dynamics and development of conflicts, and who is seeking more effective strategies to address and resolve them.

Dr. Christopher Moore
Partner, CDR Associates,
and Author of *The Meditation
Process: Practical Strategies
for Resolving Conflict*

ACKNOWLEDGEMENTS

I would like to thank the people who have supported me as I have developed, tested, and talked incessantly about these models in my work. Thank you to my business partner, Rick Russell, an outstanding mediator who helped validate many of the ideas in this book. Thank you also to Paul Emond and Julie Macfarlane, directors of the Osgoode Hall Law School Master of Laws program, where much of the research for this book was done—your support and encouragement helped a great deal. Thank you also to Rick Weiler, who introduced me to the first two models in the book and started me down this path early in my career. Finally, I'd like to thank my friend Jim Harrison, who has helped in so many ways I can't begin to express.

I would also like to thank all of the people whose work I have used to construct many of these models. Your generosity and openness in allowing me to work with and develop your material has made this book possible, and is a tribute to the core values and principles of the conflict resolution field.

Most importantly, I'd like to thank my wife, Ronalda Jones, for her unquestioning support—as the gifted writer of the family, she understood the time that was needed to do this well.

CHAPTER ONE

INTRODUCTION

Imagine for a moment that you are faced with a conflict. Imagine, for example, that your new neighbour loves to have guests over many nights of the week until the early hours of the morning, keeping you up with the noise. When you talk to your neighbour, he laughs and tells you, "Loosen up, have some fun. Come and join us if you want! You need to enjoy life more!" You go home after the conversation and get increasingly angry. You think about how insensitive he is, how little he cares for other people. You begin to think that he may actually be retaliating for the fact that your dog barks every now and then, which he complained about once. Given how you see the problem, you vow to call the police the next time he has a party during the week. This conflict is headed for a significant escalation.

We are all faced with conflict situations in many aspects of our lives, whether in our personal life, in the workplace, or with just about anyone we meet. Given how common conflict situations are and how frequently we deal with conflict, you would think that we'd all be pretty good at handling conflict.

The reality is a bit different, in that most people report little confidence in addressing or handling conflict. Why?

Managing conflict effectively is a simple two-step process that starts with:

1. how we assess the conflict we're facing, followed by
2. what action (or inaction) we decide to take to address it.

Whenever we are faced with a dispute, the first thing we do is try to make sense of it—try to determine what the conflict is about. In other words, Step One is trying to diagnose the conflict. Once we've decided on (or guessed at) the cause, Step Two is taking some type of action based directly on what we think has caused it.

In the example above, the homeowner has assessed the conflict in Step One as being caused by the neighbour's being insensitive, uncaring, maybe even vengeful. Based on this diagnosis, in Step Two the homeowner decides the reasonable and appropriate way to address this conflict is by calling the police to curtail the neighbour's uncaring, insensitive and vengeful behaviour. The conflict was assessed, and an action that seems to make sense is taken based on that assessment. But how accurate was this assessment?

In every conflict, we employ these two steps, either consciously or unconsciously. In fact, how good we are at managing conflict will be based, fundamentally, on how skilled we are at these two steps:

1. creatively and insightfully diagnosing what is causing a conflict, and
2. effectively and skillfully taking action to resolve the conflict.

In many cases, the barrier to effectively managing a conflict is that we diagnose the conflict unconsciously, react emotionally, make choices and apply tools based on a poor diagnosis, and end up escalating the situation.

WE ALL "PRACTICE" CONFLICT RESOLUTION DAILY

This is a handbook for conflict resolution practitioners aimed at helping them understand and analyze conflict more effectively in their work. Practitioners, typically, are people who regularly manage conflict as part of their work or their life. The list of practitioners, therefore, is long and includes roles such as mediators, negotiators, lawyers, managers and supervisors, social workers, human resource and labour relations specialists, insurance adjusters, and many more. For these people, this handbook introduces a number of conflict analysis models that are useful and applicable to the two steps above: diagnosing conflict, and offering direction and ideas on resolving that specific conflict.

If this book is useful to conflict resolution practitioners for the simple reason that they regularly manage conflict, what about the rest of us? In other words, who else manages conflict regularly and might benefit from using and applying some of these models? Conflict is a universal human experience, something that every single one of us works with and addresses in our lives far beyond the workplace. In that sense, we are all "practitioners" when it comes to working with conflict effectively, and the tools and models in this book will apply to everyone who wishes to improve his or her ability to manage conflict effectively. For the sake of simplicity, then, this handbook will use "mediators" and "practitioners" interchangeably to mean "people who deal with and manage conflict."

This book is focused on models and tools that help with the two key steps in managing and responding to conflict:

Step One: Effectively diagnosing a conflict, and

Step Two: Taking action to manage the conflict based on the diagnosis.

I use the term "models" frequently. This is not a call to introduce more theory or more academic understanding into the conflict resolution process. While theory and academic knowledge are excellent, they are often of little help in a given situation. If theoretical knowledge serves as the general foundation for the field, then "models" are the specific tools or heuristics that guide the application of that theoretical knowledge in practice. This handbook is not focused toward more theory, but rather on tools that can be applied directly to the practice of managing each and every conflict.

To understand this relationship between theory and practice, it will be helpful to understand the nature and characteristics of what can be called "practice professions."

DIAGNOSIS: FINDING THE ROOT CAUSES OF CONFLICT

A practice profession, quite simply, is a profession aimed at helping individual people solve specific functional problems. It is distinguished here from professions that focus more generally on research and the discovery of theoretical knowledge. There are numerous professions that have a significant practice component to them, professions as diverse as medicine and law, as well as technical professions such as civil engineering and auto repair. And the nature of every practice profession is that the first critical skill the practice professional must have is the ability to diagnose, to determine the root cause of a specific problem.

For example, when a patient sees a doctor, the first thing that the doctor must arrive at is a diagnosis of the problem; indeed, everything flows from the diagnosis, and little is done until a diagnosis is reached. During the diagnostic process, if there is any doubt about either the diagnosis or the recommended course of action (i.e., treatment) that flows from the diagnosis, a "second opinion" is often sought before any treatment is considered. Similarly in law or engineering, or even car repair, little action can be taken until the professional understands (or believes she understands) what the problem is, and based on that recommends or conducts an intervention. Few of us would accept a dentist saying, "Well, I'm not sure which tooth is hurting, so I'm going to try pulling a few of them out to see if it helps." Few of us would return to an auto repair shop that randomly replaced part after part hoping that this would eventually solve the problem.

If diagnosis is the first key ability for a practice professional, it's important to understand how the diagnostic process works and where it fits for the practitioner. In general, most diagnosis has its roots in the theoretical background knowledge of the field. For example, once a mechanic understands from automotive theory that the transmission of a car is responsible for sending power to the wheels, if a car won't move while the engine is running the mechanic starts looking at the transmission as the source of the problem. Once a doctor understands the digestive tract and what functions it performs, when a patient presents with abdominal pain immediately after eating the doctor will start investigating the digestive system first. Some theoretical knowledge is therefore necessary for good diagnostic skills.

In more complex fields, however, theory alone is inadequate for good diagnosis. In addition to a grounding in general theory, practitioners need effective models and tools to achieve an accurate and useful diagnosis. For example, heart disease is one of the most common diseases in the world. There is extensive "deep" theory and knowledge about how high levels of certain kinds of cholesterol contribute to heart disease, including complex mechanisms for how cholesterol in the blood contributes to fat slowly building up on the arterial walls, narrowing them and making the heart work too hard, eventually leading to heart attack. The theories about these mechanisms, however, are not overly helpful in diagnosing any given individual patient. To diagnose effectively, doctors have devised tests that measure cholesterol levels in the patient along with a simple model that states if cholesterol is over a certain limit, specific actions and steps are put in place to help correct the problem. The doctor, using a simple tool (a blood test) follows a specific model for diagnosing and intervening (if the cholesterol level is above a certain limit, diet changes and cholesterol medicines are prescribed) that requires very little of the deep "theory" behind the model for the practitioner to be effective in helping the patient.[1]

In general, then, theoretical knowledge is required as a foundation, but in order to apply that knowledge effectively for each individual client or situation, specific practice models and tools are required to assist the professional. These models help the practitioner apply the two key steps mentioned before:

Step One: Effectively diagnosing a conflict, and
Step Two: Taking action to manage the conflict based on the diagnosis.

Without the ability to apply appropriate models and tools effectively, there is little chance the practitioner will help the client.

THEORIES VS. MODELS IN A PRACTICE PROFESSION

We have been using the terms "theory" and "model" in specific and different ways so far, and this leads us to a key question: What is the difference between a "theory" and a "model"?

Typically, the terms "theory" and "model" are used almost interchangeably, and indeed there is overlap in their meaning.

---

1. Indeed, in many professions such as medicine and law, simpler problems that can be diagnosed with effective models and that lead to straightforward interventions are being devolved to professionals with far less theoretical knowledge, such as nurse practitioners and paralegals.

There are also some key differences, especially in the context of a practice profession.

In the Merriam-Webster dictionary the definition of "theory" includes:

- "abstract thought," and
- "a general principle or body of principles offered to explain a phenomenon," and
- "an unproved assumption."

These definitions indicate that theories are broad principles that are often related to abstract thought of a high order. Theories are strongly related to research, to the testing of hypotheses or principles to see if they are true. In the scientific method, if a theory is not verified or cannot be proven true, it is discarded as false or unusable.

This scientific approach is found in many professions (including the social sciences and conflict resolution), and is typically labeled the "research" side of the field. In the sciences, "pure," or "theoretical," or "deep" are terms used for research that initially gives little or no thought to practical uses or applications, focusing instead on uncovering foundational principles with little regard for whether they are "practical." There is a great deal of money spent and many people engaged in this type of research in many fields, including the field of conflict resolution.

Separate from the research component of most fields, there is also a "practice" or applied branch of the field centred around "practitioners," who take the existing knowledge of the field and determine how to directly apply that information to help individual patients or clients.

The term "theory," therefore, seems to point us in the direction of abstract investigation with less, or little, applicability to the practitioner. The practitioner, on the other hand, is focused on learning the clinical skills and tools that help in applying their knowledge and information directly with specific clients. For practitioners, very little "deep" theory is directly useful and applicable in a clinical setting other than in the most general way, unless the theory and knowledge has been translated into a useful functioning model.

This is precisely why many professions describe a significant split in their fields between research and practice, between theoretical work and the clinical application of that knowledge in the field. As in many fields, this significant gap between theory and practice exists because practitioners rarely see how the majority of research conducted helps them as practitioners. In many cases (though certainly not all) research is either too general or too esoteric to be easily understood, let alone directly applicable in the field. For this reason, a great deal of important information rarely (or only very slowly) makes its way to the practitioners in the field.

Models, however, can be something quite different from theory. In Merriam-Webster "model" is defined in some of the following ways:

- "a description or analogy used to help visualize something that cannot be directly observed," and
- "to produce a representation of."

Models, then, as we are using the term, have a few unique characteristics. Good models are structures or representations that approximate reality, but in a simpler and clearer way. Maps, for example, are an excellent form of model, in that they represent reality (i.e., the streets of a city), but in a smaller and simpler way (the map fits in our pocket, where the city streets themselves clearly do not), so they can help guide us to where we want to go. In the same way, conflict analysis models are "maps" of complex conflict theory or processes that are simplified and focused to help us understand the cause of the conflict in specific situations, along with the actions we might take that will help us reach a resolution.

Christopher Moore reinforces this idea that practitioners need models, or "conflict maps":

> To work effectively on conflicts, the intervener needs a conceptual road map or "conflict map" that details why a conflict is occurring, identifies barriers to settlement, and indicates procedures to manage or resolve the dispute.[2]

So how is a "model" different from a "theory"?

First, a model (unlike a theory) is not burdened with whether it is "true," but rather is burdened by the more functional test of whether it is helpful and useful in simplifying what it represents. It doesn't matter whether a model is "true" or "right" in general, it matters whether a particular model is helpful with a specific problem; if it is, we use it, and if it isn't, we don't discard it forever as "false," we simply don't use it in this situation. For example, if I am in Toronto and all I have is a map of New York, the map isn't deemed false and thrown away. It is simply not useful to me in Toronto, and I put it away until I'm back in New York, where it will once again be useful. For this reason, the experienced practitioner, like the experienced traveler, carries numerous maps that may be needed on the trip.

Second, a model helps us sift through a great deal of complex information by narrowing the focus to what will actually help us. Models, in this sense, help us take detailed theoretical knowledge and simplify it to something we can make sense of more quickly. As described by Robert and Dorothy Bolton,

> *An elegant model is a useful simplification of reality.* It enables you to ignore a mass of irrelevant or less relevant details so you can focus on what is most important. A model shows

2. Christopher Moore, *The Mediation Process: Practical Strategies for Resolving Conflict* (San Francisco: Jossey-Bass, 2003), 58.

what to look for, helps identify meaningful patterns, and aids in interpreting what you see. In other words, a model helps cut through the distracting aspects of a situation so you can better grasp the essence of what you want to understand.[3] [emphasis in original]

Models, in this sense, are tools for helping us get to the core or the root cause of the problem effectively.

Finally, models help practitioners accomplish practical goals. For example, when going to visit a friend in an unfamiliar city, we often rely on a hand-written map that our friend gives us to find her house. These maps are often poorly drawn and delete vast amounts of information about the city, concentrating only on key landmarks and streets that are directly on the way to the house. These maps are rarely to scale, and would be useless in finding anything but the friend's house. And yet, this map is a first-rate and effective model at getting us to that one location. Regardless of all its shortcomings, it is extremely practical for the specific task at hand. It is the simplest and most practical way to accomplish the goal.

Conflict analysis models, if they are effective at simplifying complex interactions as well as giving us useful guidance, should be routinely applied by practitioners in the field, and should be a core part of any practitioner's training. So how much training in this type of diagnostic model, in frameworks for analyzing and understanding the root causes of conflict, is included in most conflict resolution or mediation courses? Virtually none.

A brief look at the training outlines for a number of 40-hour mediation workshops reveals that the class time is spent in three primary areas: first, some general steps (usually four to six) on how to conduct a mediation; second, on a laundry list of conflict resolution and communication skills that are practiced individually in the workshop; and finally, role-play situations where the general mediation steps and the commu-

3. Robert Bolton, Dorothy Grover Bolton, *People Styles at Work* (New York: Amacom, 1996), 9.

nication skills are given a try. Few of these courses teach or spend time on anything resembling conflict analysis models, or even, for that matter, on the most general conflict resolution theory. Mediation training seems to be focused solely on face-to-face skills and simple steps for conducting the mediation itself,[4] and does little to teach the participants about diagnosing the root cause of the conflict being mediated.

Without the ability to translate conflict theory into models and tools that help diagnose the specific conflict at hand, and without the ability to choose actions and interventions effective for that particular conflict, practitioners will simply not be good at resolving conflict.

A WIDE RANGE OF CONFLICT ANALYSIS MODELS

There is no magic formula that resolves all disputes. Because conflict situations can be so diverse, and because models are not exclusive representations of "truth," we are not looking for a single model that will make sense of every conflict in the world. Rather, we need to be comfortable with a wide range of models that will help us in diagnosing different problems, in vastly different circumstances, with different people. This handbook contains eight different models that approach conflict situations from different points of view. All eight approaches can be useful for diagnosing and intervening in a wide range of situations.

Diagnosis is about framing the conflict in a way that has coherence and makes sense. The effective practitioner needs a wide range of diagnostic models and frameworks that help organize and make sense of a wide range of situations.

As described by Bernard Mayer, these models are essential for the practitioner:

A framework for understanding conflict is an organizing lens that brings a conflict into better focus. There are many

---

4. Some workshops, notably workshops taught out of the continuing education department of various universities, do teach some theory from the field, to their credit. Often, however, this is "theory" as defined above, and students have a hard time understanding how to apply this information in practice. Few workshops, including the university courses, teach practice-focused models of conflict analysis.

different lenses we can use to look at conflict, and each of us will find some more amenable to our own way of think-ing than others.... We need frameworks that expand our thinking, that challenge our assumptions, and that are practical and readily usable.[5]

Mayer's "lens" analogy is useful. For example, conflict can be viewed through a communications lens, a type of conflict lens, an "interests" lens, a personality lens, a structural lens, a cul-tural lens, a dynamics of conflict lens, and more. This means that an effective practitioner should have a constellation of diagnostic models to help frame and understand different sit-uations; as experience grows, the practitioner will become more skilled at choosing the one(s) that will help create effec-tive interventions.

Regardless of the type of model or map, good models do have some characteristics in common. When focusing on effective conflict analysis models, this book will present mod-els that are simple and useful. Each model needs to meet the practitioner's test: "Does applying this model help me diag-nose the problem as well as help me choose what I do next, in real time as I work with the conflict?"

The two requirements for an effective and useful conflict analysis model can be described this way:

1. **Diagnosis: Simplicity vs. Complexity**—Effective diagnostic models and tools attempt to strike a fine balance between simplicity and complexity; a model that is overly complex will be too difficult to put into practice, and a model that is shallow or obvious is a waste of time. The complexity of the diagnosis can be extreme, such as Rummel's unified theory of conflict in his book, *The Conflict Helix*,[6] which proposes a single, detailed model for understanding all conflict, all the way from the interpersonal to the geopolitical. While it may

5. Bernard Mayer, *The Dynamics of Conflict Resolution* (San Francisco: Jossey-Bass, 2000), 4.
6. R. J. Rummel, *The Conflict Helix: Principles and Practices of Interpersonal, Social and International Conflict and Cooperation* (New Brunswick, NJ: Transaction Publishers, 1991).

sound interesting to have a model that attempts to explain all conflict in the world, bear in mind that this model takes a full-length book to even explain, let alone to apply. Good models are able to address complexity, but simplify them enough to be useful.

2. **Strategic Guidance**—Effective models are clear and focused in giving strategic direction to the practitioner. The clearer the strategic direction the model gives, the more practical and applicable it becomes (and the more likely it will actually be used in conflict situations).

As you work through these eight models, keep in mind these two dimensions by asking yourself:

1. "Does it help me diagnose the conflict simply and effectively?"
2. "Does it give me direction and ideas on how to resolve it?"

BECOMING A REFLECTIVE PRACTITIONER

Another goal of the models in this book is to assist the practitioner in growing and developing, in becoming a "reflective practitioner." Reflective practice is a term that has been used by a variety of writers looking into the very nature of effective professional practice. Michael Lang and Alison Taylor's recent book is devoted to understanding the development of the mediator from novice to artist, and describes reflective practice in this way:

> Reflection is the process by which professionals think about the experiences, events and situations of practice and then attempt to make sense of them in light of the professionals' understanding of relevant theory. . . . Reflection occurs both during the performance of professional practice (reflection in action) and after the experience (reflection on action). It

nurtures exploration and discoveries that lead to an increased repertoire of skills, it enhances the person's ability to modify forms of intervention, and it may alter his way of thinking about the problems presented.[7]

Reflection, clearly, is at the very heart of the process of learning and developing, essentially the process of "learning how to learn." This process of "learning how to learn" was identified by Chris Argyris and Donald Schon as crucial to the growth of skill and ability:

> The foundation for future professional competence seems to be the capacity to learn how to learn (Schein, 1972). This requires developing one's own continuing theory of practice under real-time conditions. It means that the professional must learn to develop "microtheories" of action that, when organized into a pattern, represent an effective theory of practice.[8]

If "learning how to learn" is the path to growth, then the essential element of this growth is the ability to reflect on what is successful, what is working and what is not. And key to this would be having a framework, an ongoing set of structures or models on which to reflect and on which to base any changes or adaptations for enhanced performance. In short, practitioners need models and tools of analysis in order to become reflective practitioners.

It is important to note again that there is no single diagnostic model that is "right" or "correct" or even "true." As Folger, Poole and Stutman state,[9] theories from the practitioner's point of view (i.e., diagnostic models) are best judged by their utility, not whether they are right or wrong. They are meant to be useful, to "explain relationships so that we might

---

7. Michael Lang and Alison Taylor, *The Making of a Mediator*, (San Francisco: Jossey-Bass, 2000), 19.
8. Chris Argyris and Donald Schon, *Theory in Practice: Increasing Professional Effectiveness*, (San Francisco: Jossey-Bass, 1974), 157.
9. Many previous writers use the term "theory" in the same way we have defined the term "model," in that it refers not to deep sociological theory but rather practical frameworks that help the practitioner make sense of, or diagnose, a conflict.

describe them more fully, predict their recurring features, and control their dependant outcomes."[10]

Since they are tools and structures to help us make sense of the infinitely complex situations of conflict, the more diagnostic models and tools a mediator has the more likely he or she will understand any given conflict and intervene effectively.

> Theories should be evaluated on the basis of utility...certain concepts and theories will speak to you and others will not. . . . The real test, however, is for practitioners to employ these ideas in the marketplace of everyday life. The best theories and concepts are the ones that allow you to understand and manage conflict in your relationships, in your family, in your organization, in your life. No other measure of a theory can compete with that crucial test.[11]

It is through this process of testing, trying and getting feedback on the success and value of our diagnostic models and tools that reflective practice is achieved.

Finally, this process of reflection is also a two-way street, in that by learning and applying a model for diagnosing a situation of conflict, and by using this model to reflect on the effectiveness of the actions taken to address the conflict, the learning generated will no doubt change and improve the quality, focus and depth of the diagnostic model. It will lead, as Argyris and Schon just said, to "developing one's own continuing theory of practice," one's own models. This creates an endless process of growth, learning, and improvement in the field, practitioner by practitioner. This is the hallmark of truly effective practice.

SUMMARY

In summary, then, this book is focused on a specific type of conflict analysis model that practitioners can use to both diag-

---

10. Joseph Folger, Marshall Poole, and Randall Stutman, *Working Through Conflict*, (New York: Harper Collins College Publishers, 1993), 44.
11. Ibid., p. 67.

nose a conflict situation, as well as gain some guidance about what interventions might help and why. The key points to remember when working with these models are:

- Each model is intended to be a simple, useful map or framework to help the practitioner work with conflict situations encountered in practice.
- The range of conflict situations is virtually infinite, and one model will simply not be helpful in all situations. The practitioner should have a number of models to help with different situations.
- Conflict can be seen and addressed from a variety of viewpoints, such as communications conflict, structural conflict, personality, and many more. For this reason, too, the practitioner should have a variety of models to work with.
- Models are not looked at as "true" or "false"; they are only useful or not in a specific situation. Models that are helpful should be used. Models that are not should be put away until a situation arises where they are useful.
- Models need to meet the practitioner's test: "Does applying this model help me diagnose the problem, as well as help me choose what I do next?" Models need to be complex enough to bring value, and simple enough to be easily applied and used.
- Effective use of these models is the beginning of reflective practice, the path to continual improvement in managing and resolving conflict.

One of the most frequent comments heard from experienced practitioners exposed to these models is that they intuitively understand a number of these models, but had taken years to develop this intuition by trial and error. An important goal of learning and working with these models is to consciously speed up the practitioner's learning curve by helping everyone become a reflective practitioner. These models offer a jump-start in learning and growing as a conflict resolution practitioner.

The strategies and applications of the models described here are simply a start, a beginning, a scratching at the surface of the many ways practitioners can put these models to use. As practitioners work frequently with any of these (or other) models, they will find different ways to apply the models to their advantage; indeed, they may even adapt or modify the model to make it more useful and effective. This is only to be encouraged. This handbook is intended to introduce a basic set of models and touch on the main strategies for applying them, providing the practitioner with a useful reference manual for the ongoing use of these tools.

HOW TO USE THIS BOOK

This book is not intended to be read as a novel, from start to finish in that order. Each of the eight chapters present a specific model that is self-contained, offering a clear understanding of the model's focus, what kind of situations it can be useful in, and what interventions are likely to help. Each chapter can be read independently and stands on its own. That said, it can also be very helpful to see how the various models relate to each other, and frequent footnotes will point from one model to another where useful.

Additionally, to help the reader get a clear sense of how the different models relate to each other, there is a single case study of a complex conflict situation that all eight models are applied to. Chapter 2 starts off with this detailed case study, followed by a brief summary of all eight models. Each model will then be presented in detail in its own chapter. Within each chapter, each model is applied to the same case study, so the reader can gain an appreciation of how the model is used, and how different models will give the practitioner different viewpoints, different diagnoses, and different options for intervention. Remember that there is more than one way of assessing and intervening in a given conflict, and indeed that is one of the strengths of using different models or maps.

Each model is then followed by an additional case study unique to that chapter, to give the reader a further chance to see each model in action. Where applicable, worksheets or other helpful guides are included to round out each model.

We are all lifelong students of conflict resolution (like it or not), and hopefully one or a number of these models will become invaluable in your practice and life.

CHAPTER TWO

OVERVIEW OF THE MODELS

The Toolbox will be profiling the following eight conflict analysis models, eight different lenses or perspectives from which the practitioner can assess situations of conflict.

WHY THESE EIGHT MODELS?

There are, potentially, a lot of models, of conflict maps, that can help practitioners diagnose and intervene in conflict. So why these eight? These models were chosen for a variety of reasons. First, as models, they are especially well balanced between simplicity and complexity. The Dynamics of Trust model represents a great deal of complexity that attribution theory brings to the table, yet does so in a functional and useful way. The Triangle of Satisfaction takes the idea of interests to great depth and subtlety, yet does so in a way that can be applied in real time conflict situations.

Second, they were chosen for their clarity in giving direction and guidance for intervention. Each model offers the practitioner clear, focused ideas on what will help in the conflict, and why.

Finally, these models represent a wide range of different ways to approach and look at conflict. Each model brings a different and potentially useful angle on the problem, as follows:

- **The Circle of Conflict** looks at different causes or "drivers" to conflict;
- **The Triangle of Satisfaction** specifically looks at different types of interests, and takes that assessment to a significantly deeper and more functional level;
- **The Boundary** model looks at conflict from a unique perspective, giving insight into the almost invisible world of managing boundaries, a daily occurrence for all of us;
- **The Interest/Rights/Power** model is foundational to the field of negotiation and conflict resolution, and helps by categorizing the various processes we use to manage conflict along with the consequences of each of those types;
- **The Dynamics of Trust** model tackles the critical issue of how trust is created, how trust is eroded, and how lack of trust impacts the resolution process;
- **The Dimensions** model looks broadly at three different "layers" or areas where we can focus our work, and how those three areas affect the resolution and recurrence of conflict;
- **The Social Style** model looks at conflict through the ubiquitous personality lens, and brings clear direction on managing and resolving communication and interpersonal "style" issues;
- **The Moving Beyond** model looks at the emotional process people go through when trying to let go of conflict and move on, a critical process for achieving resolution.

This range of models is not complete, and is not intended to be. The Toolbox is intended as a foundation, a good beginning at providing practitioners with roadmaps, "conflict maps," that can assist them as they grow and develop.

Below is a very brief description of each model before moving into the individual chapters.

MODEL #1—THE CIRCLE OF CONFLICT[1]

The Circle of Conflict is a model that diagnoses and categorizes the underlying causes or "drivers" of the given conflict. It categorizes these causes and drivers into one of five categories: Values, Relationships, Moods/Externals, Data and Structure. Further, the model offers concrete suggestions for working with each of these drivers, and directs the practitioner toward Data, Structure, and the sixth category, Interests, as the focus for resolution.

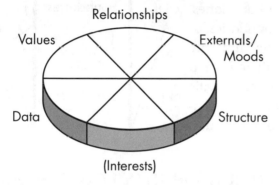

(Interests)

MODEL #2 – THE TRIANGLE OF SATISFACTION[2]

The Triangle model is an extension of the Circle of Conflict, though it easily operates as an independent framework for the practitioner. This model deepens the area of Interests, suggesting that there are three distinct types of interests: Result or substantive interests, Process or procedural interests, and Psychological or emotional interests. The model offers specific strategies for working with the three different types of interests in conflict situations.

EMOTION
(Psychological)

MODEL #3—THE BOUNDARY MODEL[3]

The Boundary model, similar to the Circle, assesses the root cause of conflict from a structural and behavioural point of view, but suggests that conflict occurs because of how people relate to and interact with boundaries. Our lives are filled with boundaries of many kinds, and may include rules, laws, contracts, cultural expectations, norms, and limits of any sort. It suggests that conflict occurs when parties disagree on boundaries, expand or break boundaries, or refuse to accept the authority and jurisdiction inherent in a boundary. It also offers specific approaches to work with conflict caused by boundary issues.

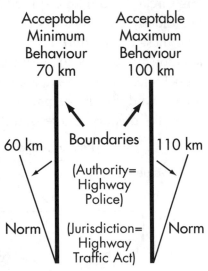

Acceptable Minimum Behaviour 70 km

Acceptable Maximum Behaviour 100 km

60 km   Boundaries   110 km

(Authority= Highway Police)

Norm   (Jurisdiction= Highway Traffic Act)   Norm

MODEL #4—INTERESTS/RIGHTS/POWER MODEL

The Interests/Rights/Power model does not assess the root causes of conflict, but rather focuses on the different processes people use to deal with conflict, categorizing all approaches to conflict as being one of three types – Interest-based, Rights-based or Power-based. The I/R/P model diagnoses the characteristics of each of the three types. Finally, the model offers broad direction on working with each of the three different processes, along with a guide for choosing effective types of processes for resolving conflict.

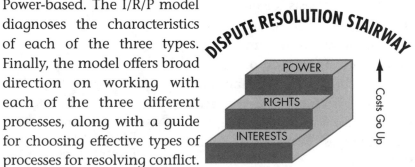

DISPUTE RESOLUTION STAIRWAY

POWER

RIGHTS

INTERESTS

Costs Go Up

3. Used with permission of Dr. Larry Prevost, Sarnia, Ontario.

MODEL #5—THE DYNAMICS OF TRUST

This model looks at the dynamics of trust and how we attribute blame. Attribution Theory, one of the most important areas of psychological research, is boiled down to help practitioners understand how trust is broken, and how blame and lack of trust can make resolution difficult if not impossible. The model also gives the practitioner specific strategies for rebuilding enough trust to facilitate the resolution process, through activities such as Confidence Building Measures (CBMs), procedural trust, and attributional retraining.

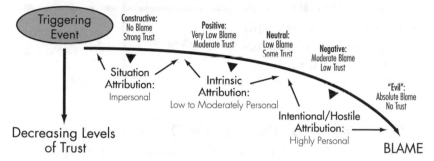

MODEL #6—THE DIMENSIONS MODEL[4]

The Dimensions model takes the broadest look at diagnosing conflict by proposing that conflict takes place along three different "dimensions." These three dimensions are the Cognitive dimension (how we perceive and think about the conflict), the Emotional dimension (how we feel about the conflict) and the Behavioural dimension (how we act or what we do about the conflict). The model identifies how separating a conflict into these dimensions can help the practitioner intervene, and offers specific strategies for working with each of the dimensions.

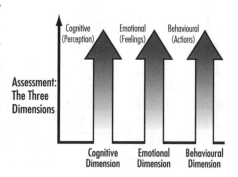

4. Used with permission of Bernard Mayer of CDR Associates.

MODEL #7—THE SOCIAL STYLE MODEL[5]

This model is significantly different from all the rest of the models because it focuses on understanding personality conflict, and conflict related to personal communication styles. Based on research similar to the Myers-Briggs Personality Type Indicator but offering a much simpler framework for assessing personal styles, the Social Style model suggests four basic personality and communication styles, or types, and offers clear skills and strategies for working with these personality characteristics in conflict situations.

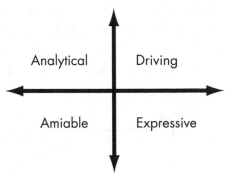

MODEL #8—MOVING BEYOND CONFLICT

One of the main barriers to resolution comes when people can't let the conflict go and move on with their lives. A dispute can become such an important part of an individual's life that he or she will not allow it to end. It feels as if something important is being lost. This is very similar to the process of grieving, and the Moving Beyond model helps identify the stages or steps parties often must go through in order to let it go and move beyond it.

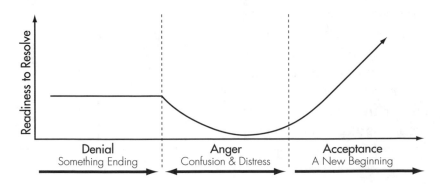

5. Social Style is copyrighted material owned by The TRACOM Group and used here with permission.

— CHAPTER THREE —

THE CONFLICT STORY: A CASE STUDY

Throughout this workbook, each of the models described will be applied to the same conflict situation to illustrate both how the model can diagnose the conflict, as well as how it can give guidance to the practitioner based on that diagnosis. The basic outline of the situation is given here.

CASE STUDY

The parties were part of a small work team in a government agency. It consisted of two clerks, Bob and Diane. Bob had been in the same position for over 12 years, with a good performance record. Diane was new, with one year in the position. They were both union members and co-equals, meaning that they had the same pay and job classification, a CL-1. They did similar tasks in the office, but for the sake of efficiency and personal interest, Bob did more accounting-type work, and Diane did more client-service-type work. The office supported a large group of professional engineers who were also union employees and reported to Sally, the manager. Bob and Diane also reported to Sally, who was new to the job as of two months ago.

After two months of settling in, Sally revealed to the whole department that she was there with a mandate to revamp the workflows, change and improve the way services were provided, and generally improve the department's slipshod performance and poor quality standards.

As she began to make changes and restructure, a number of staff members filed grievances, alleging that she was ignoring the collective agreement and requiring union members to perform tasks that were not at all related to their job classifications. Sally backed off on some of her demands, but not others, and she was not considered popular. None of the grievances had gone as far as arbitration yet.

Compounding the negative atmosphere was the fact that the organization had been negotiating a new collective agreement for the last 15 months, and it was now 12 months since the last collective agreement had expired. There was considerable frustration with senior management among the staff over this.

As part of the process, Sally announced an upgrade to one of the two clerk positions from CL-1 to an AS-1. The AS-1 role entailed a raise and was considered, in some ways, a supervisory position. The AS-1 would be responsible for most of the customer service functions, as well as assigning work to the CL-1. In addition, the AS-1 would be the interface for all communications to and from the manager, but would not be doing performance reviews of the CL-1, and would not have any authority to discipline. It was equivalent to a "team-led" position.

As with any union position, the AS-1 position was posted for competition, but was posted on short notice, and Bob and Diane were the only applicants for the position. At the end of the competition, Diane was awarded the position. Bob immediately grieved the decision, claiming that it was not conducted fairly, and that the criteria used were biased against him.

Informal meetings between Sally and the union were held about the grievance, and Sally agreed that there might have been problems with how the competition was structured. Both parties agreed that the competition would be rerun. Diane's appointment was revoked, and a new competition was run. Again, Diane and Bob applied, and this time, Diane won by a larger margin than the first time. Bob tried to file another grievance, but the union informed him that they had reviewed the process, and the competition was run in accordance with the collective agreement rules. Bob complained to the union that he was never offered "Acting" supervisor assignments by his manager (in order to develop his supervisory skills), nor given a chance to improve his customer service skills through training, and that's why he wasn't promoted. The union told him this wasn't grievable, and they couldn't help.

Bob's behaviour began to suffer. He was sullen and uncooperative with both Sally and Diane. He refused to take instructions from Diane, saying that he'd only take directions from Sally, and his behaviour fell just short of insubordination. Sally met with him and warned him that he would be disciplined if he didn't do what Diane told him. After that, his attitude got even worse. He did what he was told, but only the absolute minimum, and he did it with a negative attitude, adopting a sort of "work-to-rule" approach. The only people he spoke to at work were other staff unhappy with Sally and the changes she was making.

After about a month, he started coming in 15 to 20 minutes late every few days, and left the minute quitting time hit, regardless of who needed what. When Diane asked him about this, he simply said that other staff came in late, too. While this was occasionally true, other employees came in late a few times a year, not weekly. In addition, he told Diane it wasn't her job to discipline him, and asked to be left alone.

Diane had a very hard time dealing with Bob. She often had to ask him more than once to do a task, and if she followed up with him, he got angry. Many times, instead of telling Diane what work he had completed, he told Sally. Diane didn't know what to do, and in her frustration, she began raising her voice to Bob in a threatening manner, and occasionally used profanity.

Diane complained that she couldn't take much more of the negative attitude and behaviour. When Diane confronted Bob about this, he said that he had no problem with her, it was Sally's fault, but he was still uncooperative. Diane continued to be disrespectful, in Bob's opinion. Bob, for his part, spoke openly to other staff that Sally played favourites, that he had seniority and should have been promoted, that Sally chose Diane because they were both women, that the union was helping management shut him out, and that he was being discriminated against. While all of this behaviour was unpleasant, Bob continued doing just enough of his job to avoid serious discipline, and Sally didn't know what to do.

Bob continued to look for ways to grieve the results of the competition and promotion, but the union made it clear that they wouldn't accept a grievance on this, since they felt that the competition didn't violate the collective agreement. Bob decided to file a harassment complaint against Diane for the verbal abuse he claimed she was giving him.

— CHAPTER FOUR —

MODEL #1:
THE CIRCLE OF CONFLICT

BACKGROUND OF THE CIRCLE
OF CONFLICT MODEL

The Circle of Conflict model was originally developed by Christopher Moore at CDR Associates of Boulder, Colorado, and is a key model used by CDR in the training of mediators. This model appears in Moore's seminal mediation book, "The Mediation Process,"[1] and has been adapted with permission for this book. The version presented here is the adapted version.

The Circle of Conflict, as a model or map of conflict, attempts to categorize the underlying causes, or "drivers," of the conflict situation that the practitioner is facing, offering a framework to diagnose and understand the factors that are creating or fuelling the conflict. After offering a way to diagnose the causes of the conflict, the Circle then offers some strategic direction on ways the practitioner can move the conflict toward resolution.

---

1. Christopher Moore, *The Mediation Process*, Third Edition (San Francisco: Jossey-Bass), 2003.

DIAGNOSIS WITH THE CIRCLE OF CONFLICT

From a diagnostic point of view, the Circle of Conflict model postulates that there are five main underlying causes, or "drivers," to conflict. The model, along with the five main drivers, is as follows:

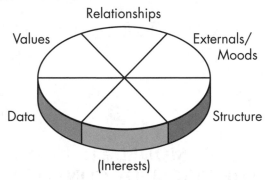

Circle of Conflict: Diagnosis

Relationships	***Values***
• negative experience in the past • stereotypes • poor or failed communications • repetitive negative behaviour	• belief systems • right and wrong • good and evil • just and unjust
Externals/Moods	***Data***
• factors unrelated to substance of dispute • psychological or physiological • "bad hair day"	• lack of information • misinformation • too much information • collection problems

Structure	
• limited physical resources (time, money) • authority issues	• geographical constraints • organizational structures

Values

The Values slice includes all the values and beliefs held by the parties that are contributing to or causing the conflict. These include terminal or life-defining values (such as religious beliefs, ethics, and morals), as well as simpler day-to-day values employed in business or work contexts (such as the value of customer service, of loyalty to the company, etc.). Value conflicts occur when the parties' differing values clash, and either cause or exacerbate the situation. Because values, morals, and ethics are so important to human beings, value conflicts tend to be very heated and personal. Examples of disputes where values play a major role include religion, abortion, and gay marriage.

Relationships

This identifies specific negative experiences in the past (past history, poor relationship) as a cause of conflict. Relationship conflict occurs when past history or experience with another party creates or drives the current negative situation. For example, if a customer had a problem with a bank over her bank account, and later finds charges on her Visa bill that she doesn't remember making, she may blame the bank right off the bat, even before finding out that the bank had nothing to do with the incorrect charges and is perfectly willing to fix the problem. Relationship problems often lead to the forming of stereotypes, lead people to restrict or end communications with the other party, and frequently lead to tit-for-tat behaviour, where one party perceives unfair treatment and retaliates against the other party; the other party then perceives this as an unprovoked attack and retaliates against the first party in some way, leading to further retaliation and conflict without end. A classic example of Relationship conflict is the feud between the Hatfields and the McCoys, where members of these two families killed each other for generations in the southern United States.

Externals/Moods

This covers external factors not directly a part of the situation, but that are still contributing to the conflict. It can be as simple as dealing with someone who "woke up on the wrong side of the bed," or who has a medical condition such as chronic back pain, which makes them cranky or difficult to deal with. It can be much more involved, such as attempting to negotiate labour contracts during a recession where neither party has caused or controls the recession, but both must deal with the negative impact of it, the negative "mood," in the negotiation. External or Mood conflict drivers occur when outside forces either cause part or all of the problem, or make a difficult situation worse. Examples include a worker with a substance abuse problem who is moody or emotional at work, or a lawyer going through his or her own divorce while trying to represent a client in a child-support lawsuit.

Data[3]

Data, or information, is identified as a key driver to conflict. Data conflict occurs when the information that the parties are working with is incorrect or incomplete, or there is an information differential—one party has important information the other party doesn't have. These Data problems often lead to further negative assumptions and further Data problems.

Another significant Data issue is the interpretation of the data, in which the parties interpret the same information in different ways. While culturally we tend to believe that "facts speak for themselves," in reality facts and information need to be interpreted, and this interpretation opens the door to significantly different views of the same information.

A good analogy is a children's connect-the-dots game. Numbered dots are printed on a page but form no obvious picture. By connecting the dots in the right order, a picture such as a dog or a house emerges. In reality, when we assess conflict

3. The Data slice is expanded and developed in the Dynamics of Trust model, specifically around Attribution Theory.

situations we are presented with the same series of "dots" or data points, only in our case without the numbering.

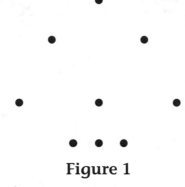

Figure 1

In Figure 1, we draw a picture by choosing to connect the dots in a particular way. The same dots, however, can be connected in different ways (i.e., different interpretations of the same information), leading to very different pictures, as in Figure 2.

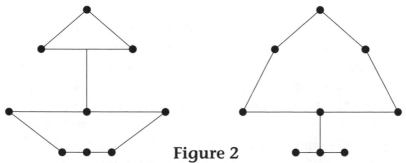

Figure 2

To complicate matters even further, now imagine that some dots (or data points) exist only in one picture, while different dots only exist in the other picture – each party has confidential information not shared with the other. Finally, as in Figure 3, it is not uncommon for a party to draw a picture that simply ignores some of the data points, since they don't fit the picture the party wants to see. Completely different pictures can then be created, each of which will be completely legitimate (even seen as exclusively "right") to the party drawing it.

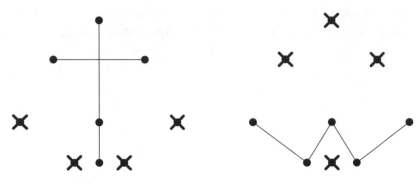

Figure 3

Structure

This covers a few different types of situations, all focused on problems with the very nature or structure of the systems we work within. Three common structural problems are limited resources, authority problems, and organizational structures.[4]

1. Limited Resources—Having limited resources in business, for example, is a structural problem caused by the competitive free-market economy that business operates within. In other words, two companies compete (often with high levels of conflict and animosity between them) because our free-market economy mandates competition as a process that all businesses must engage in. To do otherwise will violate antitrust laws. Where limited resources cause parties to compete, this is a structural cause of conflict.

2. Authority Problems—Authority problems result when people try to resolve an issue, but don't have the authority to actually make the decisions needed. At its simplest level, when you argue with a clerk in a store over an exchange or refund, it's very likely that he cannot do what you want—as a front-line clerk he is tasked with resolving customer complaints, but lacks the authority to do what you are asking.[5]

---

4. Geographical constraints, such as managing staff in remote locations or over wide geographical areas, also cause structural conflict. Since this particular driver is less common than the three listed above, I've focused on the most common examples.

5. This situation, often called "responsibility without authority," is very typical in organizations, and causes or fuels a great deal of conflict in the workplace.

This lack of authority frequently contributes to the frustration and anger the parties feel, and often leads to further escalation of the problem.

3. Organizational Structures—Organizational conflict occurs when different departments or people have to work together, but have divergent priorities for their respective work. The sales department, for example, is tasked with selling the product or service, even if it means promising things they're not sure the company can always deliver. The operations department, however, is charged with delivering the product or service in a cost-effective manner, even if it means breaching or "modifying" the promises sales has made. Each has different priorities, and this can lead to structural conflict both within the company and between the company and the client.

To better understand how the Circle can be applied as a diagnostic tool, we'll apply it to the Case Study using the five drivers.

CASE STUDY: CIRCLE OF CONFLICT DIAGNOSIS

In the case study, a number of the conflict drivers may have been at work. As we work through them, you'll note that additional information about the situation is presented; as a mediator works with a particular model or map, she will begin to explore the situation guided by the model. For our purposes, we can assume that this information came out due to the practitioner exploring these areas. A basic analysis of the situation with the Circle might be as follows:

Values

There were a number of values issues at work. First, Bob believed that he was discriminated against because of his gender, because Sally wanted a woman in that position. Diane, for her part, told the mediator she believed that Bob didn't want a woman in a position of authority over him, and that was why he refused to take direction from her. Part of these beliefs came from the fact that Diane, Sally, and two other women from another area frequently had lunch together. They regularly invited Bob and other male colleagues, none of whom ever attended, characterizing these lunches as focusing on "girl things." This reinforced the gender beliefs each of them held.

Relationships

Before any of the promotional issues arose, Diane and Bob had had an argument. Diane had questioned a few tasks Bob was responsible for, and this led Bob to tell Diane to mind her own business, she wasn't his boss. Now that Diane does indeed have some functions of a "boss" in relation to Bob, Bob thinks that Diane is holding that argument against him. The relationship has deteriorated to the point where there is now a harassment complaint against Diane, further impairing the relationship. In addition, Diane, Sally, and a few others have built a "social" relationship at work, something that Bob feels threatened by. This further strains and blocks Bob's relationship with Sally and Diane.

Externals/Moods

This organization had been recently turned into an arm's-length agency, and was no longer directly a part of the government. This had created considerable upheaval and change, which made everyone nervous and touchy. The office environment was one of suspicion and distrust toward "management," which made the issues involved here even more difficult. Finally, the fact that staff did not have a new collective agreement was upsetting employees from coast to coast, and probably contributed to the situation.

Data

There were a number of data issues. When the AS-1 position was first announced, Bob had assumed the promotion would be based primarily on seniority, and was confident he would be promoted. In reality, seniority was not a criterion that was used, and the AS-1 role was evaluated primarily on supervisory skills and "customer service" skills. Sally was not aware of Bob or Diane's career goals, and did nothing to help them plan to meet those goals. As the conflict escalated, everyone made assumptions about others' intentions, mostly incorrectly. Bob believed Sally didn't trust or like him because she was trying to eliminate communications with him. Diane believed Bob was trying to make her job so difficult she would resign the AS-1 role, so that he could have it. Bob believed that even Diane had a problem with some of the changes Sally was making. The misinformation grew rapidly.

Structure

There were a number of structural problems. First, Bob believed that Sally made these changes on her own initiative. Later, it was made clear that Head Office was implementing this CL-1/AS-1 structure in all five engineering offices across the country, and Sally had no authority or discretion to change it. Secondly, Bob didn't understand the new roles well, in that Diane seemed to be his supervisor, but didn't do his performance appraisal or any discipline. Bob couldn't see how Sally could do his performance appraisal when he wasn't allowed to interact directly with her. Diane was frustrated because she had been given responsibility for supervising Bob, but little authority to make it happen. She had to go to Sally for that authority. Finally, Sally's office was next to Diane's but down the corridor from Bob's, which meant that Sally simply got to see Diane much more often than she did Bob.

As you can see, in this case all five of the Drivers have a presence in this situation, which is not unusual. As we'll see when we look at the strategic use of the Circle, this is a fact that helps us a great deal.

Let's take a look now at how the Circle guides the practitioner toward strategic choices based on the diagnosis above.

STRATEGIC DIRECTION FROM THE CIRCLE OF CONFLICT

From a strategic perspective, the Circle tries to give the practitioner some guidance as to what to do with various types of conflict drivers once they are identified. To achieve this, the Circle is divided into two parts, the upper and lower half, with Values, Relationships, and Externals/Moods in the upper half, and Data, Structure, and Interests[6] in the lower half. Put simply, the guiding principle for the practitioner is to help the parties stay focused below the line, as this is effective in moving them toward resolution rather than escalation. The Circle does this because it asserts that you cannot directly "solve" Values, Relationship, or Mood/External issues with the other party. Since most conflicts contain a number of the drivers

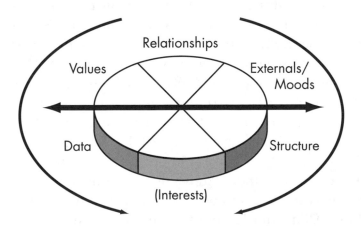

Circle of Conflict: Strategic Direction

6. Interests, for Moore and for this model, are defined as a party's "wants, needs, hopes, or fears."

identified, as practitioners we often have a lot of different drivers to work with. Strategically, therefore, the Circle guides the practitioner to focus the conflict into the Data, Structure, and Interest areas to help the parties most effectively understand and resolve the conflict.

By keeping the focus below the line on the model, parties have the best opportunity for collaborative work; by letting the focus stay on the Value differences, the Relationship problems, and the Mood/External problems that they don't control, the conflict tends to escalate and become intractable.

Some strategies in working with Data problems are:

• Have each party explain, challenge, and correct erroneous data;
• Jointly assess the data;
• Surface assumptions around the parties' assessment of data;
• Challenge assumptions made about other parties' motives;
• Jointly gather data that each party will agree to accept and rely on.

Some strategies in working with Structure problems are:

• Identify structural issues both parties face, and brainstorm solutions jointly;
• Negotiate a ratification process if authority is a problem at the table;
• Negotiate who needs to attend for both parties to most effectively resolve the issues;
• Renegotiate priorities for both parties that are more compatible and workable;
• Brainstorm ways to maximize use of scarce resources.

By far, the Interests slice is the most important area to help parties focus on. Some strategies in working with the Interests of the parties are:

- Identify the full range of interests the parties have in relation to the issues they face;
- Identify and focus the parties on their common interests;
- Look for solutions that maximize meeting each party's interests;
- Help the parties creatively solve the problems by trading low-priority interests for more important ones.

Further strategies for working with Interests will be explored in great depth with Model #2—The Triangle of Satisfaction.

CASE STUDY: CIRCLE OF CONFLICT STRATEGIC DIRECTION

In the situation with Bob, Diane, and Sally, the Circle guides the practitioner to avoid fighting over Values, Relationships, or External/Mood issues. Exploring Bob's view of female bosses, for example, or exploring Bob and Diane's argument prior to the promotion, or even exploring how the parties felt about the collective agreement negotiations would all likely result in either escalation of the conflict, or flat denials by the parties and impasse.

The Circle strategically guides the practitioner to focus the intervention into Data, Structure, and Interests. Note that each of the following strategies can be followed by brainstorming or joint problem solving to help find solutions for that issue. Presented below are some ideas on how to initiate and focus the discussions.

The following strategies should be done in the appropriate joint meeting, either with Sally and Diane, or with Bob and Diane:

Data

- Bring parties together to explain, challenge, and correct Data problems:
  - Have Sally explain the criteria for the AS-1 position, and how seniority and customer service skills were weighted in the competition. Have Bob explain to Sally his career goals, and what help he wants from her to achieve those. Have Sally outline how she can help Bob with that.
  - Surface assumptions about each other's motives:
  - Surface Bob's assumption that losing the promotion meant that his work there was not appreciated or recognized. Let Sally address this with Bob.
  - Surface Bob's assumption that Sally didn't trust him or like him because she wanted Bob to work through Diane. Let Sally explain the reasons behind the decision, and what degree of flexibility there is.
  - Surface Sally's assumption that Bob resisted change in general, even if it was change for the better. Let Bob explain his behaviour.
  - Surface Bob's assumption that Diane agreed with him and disliked Sally's changes in the work team. Let Diane explain why she supported or accepted the changes.
  - Surface Diane's assumption that Bob was trying to make her job very difficult, and let Bob explain his motives in how he behaved with Diane.
  - Surface Bob's assumption that Diane is trying to be abusive towards him when she raises her voice or swears. Let Diane explain her frustration and feelings about this, perhaps even apologizing for the behaviour.

Structure

- With Sally and Bob, identify structural issues the parties face and brainstorm solutions jointly:
    - Raise the fact that the AS-1 position was mandated by Sally's boss, and applied to all Engineering centres across the country.
    - Ask Bob to verify this at the five other centres. Let Sally talk about her degree of flexibility, and where she has discretion to make changes.
    - Raise the fact that Bob didn't understand his new role and how it related to Diane's role. Let Sally talk about how she sees the team working together, getting as specific as possible.
    - Raise the issue that Diane has been given responsibility for Bob and the area, but has little actual authority. Let Bob identify what he would need to treat Diane as his "boss," for all intents and purposes.
    - Raise the issue that Bob feels ignored by Sally, since he isn't allowed to communicate with her. Let Sally address her intentions, and brainstorm other solutions that would work for her, Bob, and Diane.
    - Surface Bob's concern that his office is farther away from Sally's than Diane's, and that this contributes to his feeling left out. Let Sally and/or Diane brainstorm ideas to improve this.

Interests

- Identify the full range of interests each person has (note that the following is a basic list, not an exhaustive one):
    - Bob wanted to do a good job, get a promotion and raise, have ongoing contact with his manager, be treated respectfully by Diane, and have a positive, constructive work environment.

- Sally wanted an end to the problems, Bob accepting her decisions and working well with Diane in a positive, constructive work environment.
- Diane wanted a good working relationship with Bob, and Bob accepting her directions in the workplace.

• Focus on Common Interests:
- All three wanted a positive, constructive work environment and an end to the problems.
- All three want to deal quickly with the harassment complaint; Bob, because he wants the behaviour to stop; Diane, because this could affect her work record; Sally, to prevent the escalation, the time it will take, and further conflict on the work team.

• Look for solutions that maximize meeting each party's interests:
- Bob could accept Diane's promotion and authority in exchange for Sally helping him work toward getting his own AS-1 position somewhere else in the company. This could include "acting" positions, training, etc.
- Sally could include Bob in the communications loop in exchange for Bob taking any problems to Diane before raising them with Sally.
- Diane could commit to respectful communications with Bob (as he defines them and as they fit into the harassment policy) in exchange for Bob being respectful (as she defines it) in accepting Diane's directions in the workplace.

Diagnosing the Case Study with the Circle of Conflict model gives the practitioner a clear understanding of the causes of the conflict, as well as a wealth of ideas for intervening that can help the parties move toward resolution.

ASSESSING AND APPLYING
THE CIRCLE OF CONFLICT MODEL

The Circle of Conflict is strong as a diagnostic model, in that it proposes specific categories for understanding the dynamics that are driving the conflict without being limited to any particular substantive type of dispute. For this reason, the Circle of Conflict can be used with just about any type of conflict a practitioner may be involved in. In addition, this tool gives the practitioner a way to identify the different causes of a conflict, and helps the practitioner look beyond the "presenting" problem to begin to question the underlying or root causes.

Strategically, this model gives clear ideas to the practitioner as to what direction to take with each "type" of conflict driver. It gives clear direction to focus away from the top half of the Circle and onto the bottom three drivers, and within that to focus on Interests above all. When working with the Data and Structure categories, it gives specific strategies for the practitioner to focus on, with an emphasis toward joint problem solving.

In terms of ease of use and applicability, the Circle strikes an effective balance between complexity and simplicity. Basically, the Circle model is simple but clear, a must for practitioners.

There are two additional conflict patterns that the Circle highlights that can be very useful to a practitioner in diagnosing conflict:

The Values/Data Dynamic

If one party to the conflict sees the conflict primarily from a Values perspective (i.e., feels that it is primarily a moral or ethical problem), and the other party sees the conflict as a Data problem, an interesting dynamic takes over. The person who perceives the problem as a Data problem will tend to give more and more information to the other party in an effort to convince them that they are right. The Values person, of course, is very unlikely to change their mind based on more data (and are unlikely to even read the data!). The conflict is likely to escalate rapidly, with the Data person accusing the Values person of bad faith ("I keep giving you important and relevant information, and you just ignore it!"), while the Values person will start to consider the Data person unethical or unprincipled ("What kind of person would try to rationalize this kind of decision?!"). The real problem, of course, is that they are actually dealing with two different problems, and are unaware of that fact. If this happens, the conflict will migrate to the top half of the Circle fairly quickly, landing on the Values and/or Relationship drivers, two of the hardest to resolve.

The Structure/Relationships Dynamic

Suppose two individuals, A and B, work in different departments, and A needs a report from B to complete his work. For B, this is a low priority, but for A, it is very high. This is a structural problem, in that A has no authority to order or direct B to do what he needs. For the first few days, A will accept B's promise that he'll "get to it as soon as possible." After a week or two goes by without getting the report from B, A will stop thinking that B's problem is a lack of time, and will start to personalize it, saying, "The problem isn't B's time, he's had two weeks! The problem is B; he doesn't want to help me." And rather quickly A and B will no longer just have a Structural problem, it will become a Relationship problem—and much harder to solve.

As with all models, we are not concerned with proving that the Circle of Conflict model is "right" about the Case Study presented, but rather asking the question, "Does it help us work with the people and the situation?" The answer is yes, as it gives practitioners a clear and simple framework for both understanding what is causing or contributing to the conflict, and what might be done to move forward constructively.

PRACTITIONER'S WORKSHEET FOR THE CIRCLE OF CONFLICT MODEL

1. Diagnose and list the causes of your conflict situation using the Five Drivers: Values, Relationships, Moods/Externals, Data, and Structure.

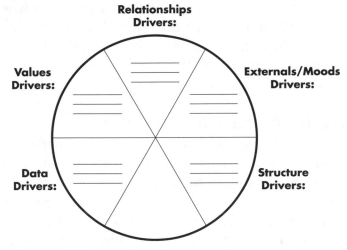

2. Develop a full list of each party's Interests (wants, needs, fears, hopes):

Party A:	Party B:
Interest:	Interest:
•	•
•	•
•	•
•	•
•	•

3. Guide the intervention to focus on the bottom half of the Circle—Data, Structure, and Interests:

Data Strategy Questions:

What Data is different between the parties?	
What Data can be collected jointly?	
What "connect-the-dots" assumptions or interpretations are the parties making about the Data?	
What assumptions about other parties' motives are being made?	
What Data substantiates the assumptions?	
What Data contradicts the assumptions?	
Other Data issues:	

Structure Strategy Questions:

What limited resource problems are the parties facing? What other resources can the parties bring to the table?	
Where is lack of authority a significant problem? What process can be used to address the lack of authority?	
How divergent are the parties' priorities? What is the process for aligning the parties' priorities?	
Other Structure issues:	

Interest Strategy Questions[7]:

What is the full range of the parties' Interests?	
Given the parties' full range of interests, what are their Common Interests?	
Where can the parties "dovetail" their Interests?	
Other Interests issues:	

4. Other Strategies Suggested by the Circle of Conflict:

- If the dispute is stuck in **Values**:
    - Have the parties share information about their values,
    - Look for common or "superordinate" values the parties share. Focus on the common values as a way of minimizing the competing values,
    - Separate areas of influence, so that one party runs the finances, and the other handles operations, for example,
    - Agree to disagree on values, and shift discussion to the parties' Interests, i.e., what they want given that they have competing values,
    - Gently uncover incongruous values held by a party.

7. For in-depth strategies for Interests, see Model #2, The Triangle of Satisfaction.

- If the dispute is stuck in negative **Relationship** issues:
  - Take a "future focus," and help them look at what needs to change to improve the situation; a past focus tends to focus on blame,
  - Help them develop a vision of the ideal future and brainstorm with them how they can get there,
  - Find out specifically what each party needs to see from the other party to change their perception of them. Help them commit to making those changes,
  - Focus them on their interests, and what they need to get past the Relationship issues,
  - Help them agree to small steps that will build trust, and begin to change their perceptions of each other in the relationship.[8]

- If stuck in **Externals/Moods**:
  - Acknowledge the external issues that they don't control, and focus them on what they do control and/or influence,
  - Find a way to bring the people who do control the External influence into the negotiation, if appropriate,
  - Help each party plan to deal with the External issue separately, and limit the negotiations at the table to the issues between the parties,
  - Reconvene when the Mood or External issue has diminished,
  - Focus them on their Interests, given that they don't control the External issues.

ADDITIONAL CASE STUDY— CIRCLE OF CONFLICT

An additional case study follows, along with how the Circle of Conflict could be applied by the practitioner.

---

8. See the Dynamics of Trust model to explore the trust issues in greater depth.

Case Study: The Spanish Estate

The conflict was caused by the passing of an elderly, first-generation Spanish immigrant. He left four children—the oldest daughter, Anne; the second oldest, Maria; the third oldest, Joe; and the youngest, Angie.

In the father's final years he needed care, and only the second oldest, Maria, took on the task, moving into the father's house with her husband and two kids. She took care of him for over seven years, and apparently angry that she was the only one caring for the father she restricted the visiting rights of her siblings. The other three children filed a lawsuit demanding, and getting, more access to spend time with the father. The son was most estranged from the father, although he visited once in a long while. Relations between Maria and the other three continued to deteriorate, culminating in the disappearance of an expensive set of tools that Joe had acquired and stored in the father's garage. Maria had information that the tools had been stolen by Joe for the insurance money, but Joe denied this and sued Maria in small claims court, saying that Maria sold the tools. This dispute was still ongoing.

The father passed away, leaving a will that split everything equally between the four children. The estate comprised the father's house, four properties back in Spain (some owned communally with other relatives), personal jewellery of the mother and father (and other effects), and about $50,000 in cash. Maria claimed some of the jewellery was given to her by the mother (who had died nine years before), along with a statue of the Virgin Mary. The other three disputed that she was "given" this. Other jewellery was simply missing; Maria claimed the parents lost it, while the siblings thought Maria had taken it. Finally, the father had made various loans to all four children, with no records or provision that they needed to be repaid to the estate. The children had stopped speaking to each other, and the three children filed a lawsuit to freeze the estate until an agreement could be reached.

Circle of Conflict Diagnosis: The Spanish Estate

Values

There were a number of values dynamics. In traditional Spanish culture, according to the three children, the oldest sibling was entitled to make decisions for the whole family. When the oldest daughter tried to do this, Maria ignored her and said that in North America, this traditional approach wasn't acceptable. The three children were offended that Maria was renouncing part of their shared cultural past. In addition, Maria was very religious, and since she believed that Joe had stolen the tools stored in the father's garage, it was hard for Maria to even speak to Joe—she viewed him as nothing but a liar. Finally, Maria saw that she was the only one who had stepped forward and cared for the father; according to her, she had had to step into the eldest child's role, according her the status of eldest. The other three rejected this.

Relationships

There were a number of Relationship dynamics. When Maria took the father in, according to the other three, she refused to let them see him. This got worse and worse, and about three years before the father died, they filed a lawsuit against Maria for access and visitation with the father. After both sides spent money on lawyers, there was a negotiated agreement for access. This episode effectively ended communication between the three siblings and Maria.

Externals/Moods

There were a few External/Mood dynamics. The family was still intimately involved and connected to the extended family in Spain, and both Maria and the three siblings had family members that they spoke with in Spain. In addition, these family members tended to talk about the conflict with others in the extended family, "stirring it up," which fuelled the conflict in North America.

Data

There were a number of Data issues. The primary one was the value of the father's house. This was a large house in a significant state of disrepair. They had "valuations" done by two local real estate agents, one suggesting listing the property at $275,000, the other at $325,000. There were wildly different assessments for the cost of needed renovations, none of them from licensed contractors. In addition, Maria claimed that the foundation was cracked, and that alone would cost $30,000 or more to repair. Joe claimed he watched the home sales in the area, and said that if it were fixed up, due to its size, it would sell for over $500,000, maybe even $550,000. Another data issue was the value of the properties in Spain, especially important since the siblings did not want to sell them but simply to value them then divide them up. A final data question was the level of the father's competency in the final two years. Had he been competent to make the financial decisions that he made, which apparently benefited Maria?

Structure

There were two key Structure dynamics. First, Maria lived in the father's house, and controlled access to the contents, inspectors, etc. When he was alive, the other siblings claimed that she controlled the father's finances as well, by virtue of the fact she lived there. The other structural problem was that the laws in Spain are different from laws here, and if an agreement was reached here, it would not necessarily be binding on properties in Spain. Finally, the whole estate was only worth somewhere around $500,000, and if the siblings litigated all of the issues, most of that would be spent on legal fees before the siblings received any of the money.

CIRCLE OF CONFLICT WORKSHEET: THE SPANISH ESTATE

This is how the Circle of Conflict Worksheet might look:

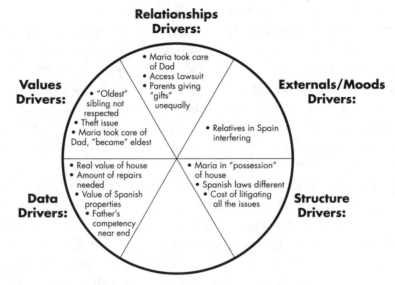

Circle of Conflict Strategic Direction: The Spanish Estate

The Circle guides the practitioner to focus on the bottom part of the Circle, into Data, Structure, and Interests. Following the guidelines, it might look like this:

Data Strategy Questions:	Possible Intervention Action:
What Data is different between the parties? • Main issue: value of the house, and cost of repairs needed.	• Get full appraisal of property, either jointly or two separate ones. Also, get contractor(s) to estimate what repairs will cost.

Data Strategy Questions:	Possible Intervention Action:
• Second issue: value of Spanish properties.	• Gather information from Spanish relatives as to how value can be established.
What Data can be collected jointly?	• See above; both could be done jointly.
What "connect-the-dots" assumptions or interpretations are the parties making about the Data? What assumptions about other parties' motives are being made? • Everyone assuming data that is in their interests to assume, such as house value. • Siblings are assuming Maria is withholding personal effects, jewellery, etc. • Siblings assuming father was not competent when he gave anything to Maria. • Maria assuming that siblings are out to get her at all costs.	• Question both parties carefully to flesh out what they think. Some can be done in plenary, some should be done in caucus.
What data substantiates the assumptions? • Little—mostly hearsay and interpretation.	• Challenge the parties (gently) to back up their claims with data, if they can. Highlight the assumptions and "beliefs." • Ask them what data would change their beliefs about the other party.

(Continued)

Data Strategy Questions:	Possible Intervention Action:
What data contradicts the assumptions? • Maria produced some jewellery, some of it more valuable than the missing jewellery. • Siblings offered to let Maria keep some of the personal effects, if others were made available to the three of them.	• Reality-test the parties, such as: • Ask the siblings, "If Maria were simply stealing it, why wouldn't she steal the most valuable items? Why would she produce any at all?" • Ask Maria, "If they are out to get you at all costs, why are they offering to let you keep some of the jewellery? Why wouldn't they demand it all?"
Other Data issues:	

Structure Strategy Questions:	Possible Intervention Action:
What limited resource problems are the parties facing? What other resources can the parties bring to the table? • While the estate has some money, it will be quickly spent. Also, nothing can come from the estate until an agreement or resolution is found. • Can any family members in Spain, whom both parties trust, be enlisted to help?	• Gain agreement from the parties on procedural matters to reduce legal fees for everyone. • Explore appointing a Spanish relative to value the properties in a way that all four children agree is fair.

Structure Strategy Questions:	Possible Intervention Action:
Where is lack of authority a significant problem? What process can be used to address the lack of authority? • Maria's husband had a huge influence on the out-come for Maria, but was not at the table.	• Frequent breaks for Maria to phone her husband helped keep him in the loop. • Arranging for the lawyer to talk to the husband directly late in the negoti-ation helped Maria agree to a deal.
How divergent are the par-ties' priorities? What is the process for aligning the par-ties' priorities? • Priorities were both aligned and divergent. Priorities centred around each party trying to "get" the other one, and on getting this over as quickly as possible.	• Highlight early on the two choices, of trying to "get" each other vs. getting this done quickly. Offer them a choice, and hold them accountable for that choice during the negotiations.
Other Structure issues:	

Interests:

Party A: Three Siblings	Party B: Maria
• Want most value for house • Want fair split of whole estate • Want Anne to make deci-sions about personal effects, as oldest sibling	• Wants to buy the father's house for as little as possi-ble, and live there • Wants to honour parents and their legacy

(Continued)

Party A: Three Siblings	Party B: Maria
• Want to honour parents and their legacy • Want parents' hard work to earn money honoured, not squandered by the children on lawsuits • Want to punish Maria for taking advantage of father • Want Maria to get no more than her fair share • Want to spend as little on lawyers as possible • Want to stop fighting • Want to stop damaging the family any further • Want to look reasonable to extended family	• Wants acknowledgement for all the work taking care of the father • Wants to stop fighting • Wants this over, so they can stop fighting • Wants to stop feeling "ganged up" on • Wants to keep personal effects given to her by parents • Wants religious values of honesty and family upheld • Wants to minimize damage to the family relationships • Wants to spend as little as possible on lawyers • Wants parents' hard work to earn money honoured, not squandered by the children on lawsuits

Common Interests

Both parties want some or all of the following:

• Want fair split of whole estate
• Want to honour parents and their legacy
• Want parents' hard work to earn money honoured, not squandered by the children on lawsuits
• Want everyone to get their fair share

- Want to spend as little on lawyers as possible
- Want to stop fighting
- Want to stop damaging the family relationships any further
- Want to look reasonable to extended family

Other Strategies:

- What are the superordinate values, such as honouring the father's memory, that they can focus on?
- What do they want from family relationships in the future? What can they do today to assist with that (future focus)?
- What interests dovetail effectively for trade-offs in the negotiation?
- How can each party recognize what the other has been through, even if they don't agree on the choices made?
- All siblings have a common experience, having lost their father. How might recognizing this help them work a bit better together?

Epilogue of the Case Study: The Spanish Estate

The mediator focused the parties below the line, and they reached agreement very quickly on:

The Spanish properties: It was agreed to remove them from the North American settlement and to deal with them over in Spain, with the stated agreement that the value, however agreed by them all, would be shared four ways equally. This reduced the complexity, and left them to be addressed under Spanish rules and law.

The house: It was agreed that Maria could buy the house, but only if she paid fair value. The process for establishing fair value was explored in detail, including the obtaining of two appraisals by qualified appraisers. After much discussion and looking at the time and expense, the siblings finally decided that they would buy the house for $325,000 if offered, so if Maria wanted it for that, she could have it. This was the equivalent of getting $344,500 on the open market, less commission, and they felt they could accept that. Otherwise, it would simply be sold and split equally. Maria spoke with her husband, and decided that while it was more than she wanted to pay, to keep the family home in the family she would buy it for that amount. (Data wise, it was also made clear that the increase from the $300,000 Maria offered to the $325,000 she paid was only $18,750, since she received 25 percent of any increase in price through her share of the estate.)

The personal effects: It was agreed by the siblings in caucus that there was no way of ever finding out if Maria was lying or not, so to help end the fighting they would divide up the personal effects that were available. Maria and the siblings agreed that they should each choose one item in order of birth, so Anne first, then Maria, then Joe, then Angie. This honoured the eldest with the first choice, and Maria accepted this. They all made their choice, and agreed to the same process with all the rest of the contents of the house.

By keeping the focus below the line, by reinforcing the common interests throughout, the parties were able to stay on track and reach an acceptable resolution.

CHAPTER FIVE

MODEL #2:
THE TRIANGLE OF SATISFACTION

BACKGROUND OF THE TRIANGLE MODEL

The Triangle is actually a related part of the Circle of Conflict, and is taken from the same source, Moore's book *The Mediation Process*. It is, in essence, a deeper layer for analyzing the concept and idea of interests, an idea that is fundamental to the entire conflict resolution field.

DIAGNOSIS WITH THE
TRIANGLE OF SATISFACTION

Remembering that "interests," for the purposes of these first two models, are defined as a party's "wants, needs, fears, hopes or concerns," the Triangle suggests that there are three broad *types* of these interests. Further, the Triangle proposes that we can map all interests into these three different types, and that these three types are qualitatively different from each other. When working to resolve conflict with the parties, each type of interest requires different interventions and different approaches to be successful.

Graphically, the model of the three types of interests looks like this:

EMOTION
(Psychological)

The Triangle of Satisfaction

Result (or substantive) Interests

This is the "what," the outcome, the most tangible part of a conflict. In litigation, who pays how much money to whom; on a work team, what the final decision is on a contentious issue; in a landlord/tenant issue, whether the tenant keeps the apartment, what the new rental amount is, etc. These are all Result or substantive interests.

For example, in purchasing a house, the main Result interest of the purchaser might be the lowest final purchase price and inclusion of as many light fixtures, appliances, and curtains as possible. The main Result interest of the seller might be the highest price in "as is" condition.

Process (procedural) Interests

This is the "how," the process by which we reach a result. *When* the solution is implemented, *how fair* the process is, *how inclusive* the process is, *how transparent* the process is, *who* is involved in the negotiation or decision-making process, are all Process or procedural interests.

Following our house purchase example, some Process interests might be *who* presents the offer (the agent or the buyer himself), *how fair* the negotiation process has been (has the buyer "low-balled" on their first offer, angering the seller? Has the seller threatened to pull it off the market if they don't like the offer? Is there a "bidding war" for the property, or is this the only offer in sight?), *how long* the contingencies for financing or inspection are, and so on.

Emotion (psychological) Interests

This is what is going on emotionally or psychologically as we try to reach an agreement. Wanting to "win," to save face, wanting to be heard, issues of status or self-worth, quality of the relationship, wanting an apology or wanting revenge, feeling satisfied—these are all psychological or Emotional interests parties may have.

In our house-buying example, one psychological or Emotional interest may be the question of who gets the antique chandelier; for the buyer it makes the house seem unique and special, while for the seller it was her grandmother's and has great emotional value. It may be worth little on the market, but it may make or break the deal, since the parties are emotionally attached to it far beyond the substantive value. In other situations, which party accepts the other's "final offer" may represent who "won" the negotiation in their minds, and since neither party will want to feel like they lost the negotiation, no deal is struck. Wanting to meet a buyer personally to know the home went to "nice people" may be important from an Emotional perspective.

The Triangle is used diagnostically on an ongoing basis to assess which type of interest is most important for each party at each point in time. This can be quite important, since people change their interests, or shift the emphasis of what is important within their interests, as a regular part of the conflict resolution process.

CASE STUDY: TRIANGLE OF SATISFACTION DIAGNOSIS

In our Case Study, we can apply the Triangle to assess and understand the interests of the parties. As we work through this, you'll note new information appearing. This is because any practitioner who works with this model will be aware of these different types of interests, and will go out of her way to uncover, explore, and understand the full range of the parties' interests.

Applying the Triangle to our Case Study, the interests might look this way:

BOB'S INTERESTS:	
Result Interests:	• Bob wants a promotion and raise in pay, either this promotion or another one; • Bob wants "acting" assignments offered to him; • Bob wants support and help improving his skills.
Process Interests:	• Bob wants access and interaction with Sally; • Bob wants fairer criteria for selecting the AS-1; • Bob wants what he sees as discrimination to stop; • Bob wants Sally to assign the tasks, not Diane; • Bob wants this all resolved quickly; • Bob wants to avoid any discipline for his behaviour; • Bob wants to keep his job.

Psychological Interests:	• Bob wants Sally punished for her poor treatment of him; • Bob wants Diane to stop her disrespectful behaviour toward him; • Bob wants recognition for his 12 years of good service in the area; • Bob wants to feel he has some control over the changes affecting him; • Bob wants a positive, constructive work environment; • Bob wants Diane and Sally to acknowledge he is a good worker who contributes to the team.

SALLY'S INTERESTS:	
Result Interests:	• Sally wants Diane to keep the AS-1 position; • Sally wants Bob to be a productive, happy team member; • Sally wants to offer Bob "acting" assignments, if he demonstrates the skills and attitude needed; • Sally would like to help Bob develop his interpersonal skills.
Process Interests:	• Sally wants a quick resolution to all these problems; • Sally wants to spend less time managing these employees; • Sally wants most communications channelled through Diane (but is willing to include Bob in the loop for information); • Sally wants Bob to have input and involvement in task assignments, but to have him accept and listen to what Diane tells him;

(Continued)

Process Interests:	• Sally wants to avoid any need for disciplining Bob for his behaviour, as that isn't good for morale; • Sally wants Diane and Bob to resolve the harassment complaint before it goes any further.
Psychological Interests:	• Sally wants Bob to admit he behaved badly; • Sally wants Bob to recognize and accept her authority to make these changes; • Sally wants Bob to hear that she appreciates his 12 years of service with a good performance record; • Sally wants Bob to have a positive and constructive attitude at work; • Sally wants Bob to have a proactive attitude toward his job, and take ownership and initiative in the workplace; • Sally wants Bob to feel in control of some of the changes, but within the parameters she sets; • Sally wants Bob to understand that she is not discriminating against anyone in the workplace.

DIANE'S INTERESTS:	
Result Interests:	• Diane wants to stay in the AS-1 position; • Diane wants Bob to accept her direction; • Diane wants Bob to drop the harassment complaint.
Process Interests:	• Diane wants Bob to have input into his tasks, rather than her ordering him to do anything;

Process Interests:	• Diane wants Bob to come to her with problems before going to Sally, so she can try to solve them first.
Psychological Interests:	• Diane wants a positive, constructive work environment; • Diane wants to feel good about coming in to work; • Diane wants Bob to have a positive, helpful attitude toward her; • Diane wants Bob to accept her as the AS-1.

There are a few things we can see from the Triangle analysis. First, it requires the practitioner to develop a fairly deep understanding of what is motivating the parties by exploring and understanding their interests. Interests, fundamentally, are what motivates every person to do what they do, to take the actions that they take. Motivation, essentially, is the parties' wants, needs, fears, concerns, and hopes; by assessing and understanding these well beyond the superficial level, the practitioner can gain critical insight into what will be needed for the parties to reach resolution.

Second, as even a cursory read of the interest analysis shows, there are significant areas of "common interest" that can be developed as a foundation for resolution. All human relationships are a mix of common interests and competing interests, and the Triangle helps the practitioner map or understand that dynamic effectively. Thirdly, what we don't know from this analysis yet is the real priority of any of those interests, what are deal-breakers and what are simply "nice-to-haves." While we can certainly get a sense of what is important to each party through the Triangle analysis, it's only through the negotiation and resolution process itself that we will discover each party's true priorities.

STRATEGIC DIRECTION FROM
THE TRIANGLE OF SATISFACTION

The next step is to consider what the practitioner can do is based on the Triangle diagnosis.

Strategy #1: Focus on Common Interests

The practitioner needs to identify and work with the parties around their common interests. Remember, every relationship has a dynamic mix of both common and competing interests. The special nature of conflict, however, is that parties in a conflict will tend *to ignore all common interests in order to focus on the competing ones* and, further, will tend to focus on the hottest, most provocative competing interest they can find. This is a normal human tendency that unfortunately leads directly to escalation, not resolution. The mediator's role is to help the parties recognize the common interests that exist in the situation (that exist in *every* situation), and use those common interests as a basis for resolving the conflict.

Finally, the practitioner can explore the apparent competing interests to see if there's a common interest underlying the competing interests. For example, on a competing interest around money (one wants more, the other wants to pay less), the common interest may be payment schedules (both want the payment later, the payer for cash flow reasons, the payee for tax reasons). Frequently, competing interests that appear on the surface are obscuring a deeper common interest that can help both parties.

Strategy #2: Work with the
Three Types of Interests Differently

A critical part of the Triangle model is the idea that the practitioner needs to help the parties address all three types of interests to get a good outcome. In addition, each of the three types of interests requires a different approach and different intervention skills.

- Result Interests can be solved, or resolved. They are typically tangible issues that can be negotiated in very direct, hands-on ways. This can happen through a variety of approaches— brainstorming, collaborative problem solving, BATNA (Best Alternative To a Negotiated Agreement) analysis and strengthening, competitive bargaining, or compromise. Either way, however, Result interests require a tangible, substantive solution acceptable to all parties.

- Process Interests tend not to be "solved" so much as negotiated on an ongoing basis. As we work to find a full resolution, the process often has to be changed and/or reinvented. The practitioner must think outside the "content" of the problem and keep an eye on the structure of the process itself. Substantive problems may change the Process by requiring technical experts to attend and have input; timing issues may call for a speeding up or slowing down of the process. Psychological interests may require the symbolic attendance of senior executives. Fairness may have to be demonstrated to all parties through disclosure of seemingly irrelevant data. The Process must constantly be re-evaluated to ensure that the Process being used is helping the parties move forward effectively.

- Psychological Interests are never "solved." They are often people's feelings, and feelings cannot be bargained away or compromised. Psychological interests must be expressed, listened to, acknowledged, processed, and finally let go when they are satisfied. Emotional/Psychological interests need to be addressed respectfully and directly, and must be treated as importantly as the other two types of interests if they are to contribute to a final resolution.

Strategy #3: Move the Parties
Around the Triangle to Avoid Impasse

The practitioner needs to use the Triangle to work through impasse. Impasse is what stops parties from solving their problems, and impasse can be caused by parties getting stuck on any of the three types of interests. The practitioner needs to effectively move parties around the Triangle, shifting the focus to different types of interests at different times to help all parties see the full range of their own interests.

Triangle of Satisfaction: Strategic Direction

In many circumstances, the resolution of one type of interest comes from focusing on and working with one of the other types of interests.

Process Solutions to Results Impasse

Sometimes, when the Result appears incompatible, parties can agree on a process to determine the Result. They might let a third party decide the Result (arbitration). Commercial real estate disputes about fair lease rates are often resolved by having each party obtain a professional appraisal, and then averaging the two results. They agree up front to a fair process, and accept the solution (Result) that the process delivers.

Result or Process Solutions to Psychological Impasse

If parties are stuck because of deep mistrust between them, one party may unilaterally give the other party a small part of the Result they are demanding as a confidence-building measure (CBM[1]). This is a Result solution to the Psychological problem of low trust. Another confidence-building measure is allowing a third party to verify that each party is adhering to the agreement. By building a Process solution (independent verification) into the Psychological problem of low trust, parties can continue to interact. Over time, as each side sees the other behaving in a trustworthy fashion, the need for the Process step of verification diminishes and trust builds. This can be a Process solution to the Psychological problem of low trust.

Psychological Solutions to Result or Process Impasse

Sometimes, when the impasse is either substantive or procedural in nature (parties stuck on the outcome or the money, or refusing to even discuss certain issues), the mediator can guide them to seeing the issues a bit from each other's perspective. This may mean having each party talk about the impact of the conflict on them personally, how it feels, what it has done to their family or their business or their life. Helping to build some understanding and recognition between the parties (not agreement, just acknowledgment) humanizes each to the other, and may lead to more flexibility in the process and in the results the parties will consider.

Process Solutions to Psychological Impasse

If parties are so angry with one another that they cannot even meet, one solution is to have all communication and interaction take place through an acceptable third party acting simply as a conduit, not a decision-maker. This allows parties to deal with issues, but in way that prevents direct contact until the Emotional side is cooled off enough to allow it. This

---

1. Please see the Dynamics of Trust model for more strategies around trust-building and CBM's.

Process of "shuttle diplomacy" is an effective way to deal with the Emotional issues that are blocking resolution.

Clearly, by looking at the three different types of interests at play in any situation of conflict, the practitioner has greater understanding of the motivation and behaviour of the parties. Based on this analysis and diagnosis, a great many new interventions are readily apparent.

Let's take a look at how the Triangle can be used strategically in our Case Study.

CASE STUDY: TRIANGLE OF SATISFACTION STRATEGIC DIRECTION

Once the full range of the parties' interests have been fleshed out through the diagnostic use of the Triangle, the practitioner needs to make some decisions about what to do with these interests. In reviewing the interests, it becomes clear that the main interests seem to be focused between Bob and Sally, with Diane and Bob having a more limited set of interests (though no less important). Since many of the interests seem related to the relationship between Sally and Bob, below are two possible steps the practitioner can use to intervene:

Step One

Use the first strategy, Focus on Common Interests. The mediator brings Bob and Sally together to confirm and reinforce their common interests, as well as to explore what appears to be competing interests. In doing this, Bob and Sally recognize that they both want at least some of the following:

• Both want Bob to take on "acting" assignments, if he demonstrates a capability and attitude for this;
• Sally is willing to help Bob develop his skills in this regard.

- Both want Bob to have at least some access and interaction with Sally (level of this to be defined);
- Both want the conflict between them resolved quickly, as it's unpleasant for everyone;
- Both want to avoid this going through a disciplinary process;
- Both acknowledge Bob's long and solid service record to date;
- Both are willing to have Bob in the communications loop directly with Sally (though this must not add extra time for Sally);
- Both want Bob to have some input and control over the changes going on (though this needs to be within defined parameters);
- Both want a positive, constructive work environment;
- Both want the harassment issue with Diane resolved;
- There appears to be a hot competing interest in that Bob wants Sally punished and Sally wants Bob to admit that he behaved badly. In exploring this, however, the practitioner finds a common interest—both want to be treated respectfully in the workplace, and to have the unwanted behaviour stopped. What appears to be a competing interest can actually be framed and developed as a common interest.

The mediator, in working through these common interests, sets a foundation of hope with the parties that these issues can actually be resolved.

Step Two
Use the second and third strategies, Work with the Different Types of Interests Differently, and Move the Parties Around the Triangle to Avoid Impasse.

Psychological Interests
It was clear from the meetings that the Psychological interests for Bob were very strong. In the first meeting, after fleshing out

the common interests, the mediator asked Bob to describe how he was feeling about the last few months at work. Bob responded with statements like, "Discriminated against, no value to my work, they're trying to force me to quit, the last 12 years thrown away, being abused by Diane for standing up for my rights," and so on. The mediator asked Sally to describe the workplace. Sally talked about how Bob's resistance and attitude affected her and others, and how disrespectful she felt his lack of cooperation was, even though she agreed that abuse of any kind was unacceptable. The mediator asked Sally to talk about how she viewed Bob overall. She spoke of Bob's strengths, what Bob was good at, what Bob could improve, his strong service record, and overall how he had been a real asset to the organization. While this seemed to help, Bob then replied, "If you think I am such a good employee, why didn't I get the promotion?" This allowed the mediator to shift from Psychological to Process interests.

Process Interests
The mediator shifted to Process interests by asking Bob how well he understood the competition system, why the union thought it was fair, why management would have bothered re-running the competition if they just wanted to shut Bob out, how common it was in the workplace for people to not succeed in their first few competitions, etc. Bob replied that he didn't really understand the competition system since it was the first one he had applied for, but that Sally should have helped him with it. The mediator also asked Bob what he wanted done differently in the future, and Bob said that while he wanted the promotion, he also wanted more contact with Sally, her help in preparing for any other job openings for AS-1's that came up, and to be included more in the information loop. Sally stated that she was open to all of that, if his attitude and behaviour changed. This opened the door for a shift to Results.

Result Interests

The mediator clarified that Bob wanted to apply for other AS-1 positions, and Bob replied he definitely would. The mediator asked Sally if she could help him with that. Sally stated that she could help by offering "acting" roles and by sending Bob on appropriate training, but only if Bob demonstrated constructive behaviour and initiative. Bob agreed, and they discussed and listed specifically how Bob would demonstrate this to Sally, after which Sally would begin offering "acting" roles. This gave Bob clear goals to work on, ones that would help him get specific things from Sally. This shift to the Result interests is now starting to define a "solution" that might work for both.

From a strategic point of view, the practitioner guided the discussions through the three different types of interests and worked with each one in a way appropriate for that particular type:

- Psychological interests were approached through helping the parties listen and acknowledge what they were hearing.
- Process interests were addressed by exchanging a lot of information between the parties, and joint problem solving developed a process that met both their interests.
- Result interests were gently bargained, meaning Sally offered to give Bob what he wanted (acting roles, training) if he gave her what she wanted (demonstration of initiative and constructive choices).

In steps 1 and 2 above, the practitioner applied all three strategies suggested by the Triangle.

ASSESSING AND APPLYING THE TRIANGLE OF SATISFACTION MODEL

Diagnostically, the Triangle is focused on analyzing the specific interests of each party. Since Interests are present for all people in all situations, this model can be applied effectively in virtually every conflict situation. In defining and relating the three different types of interests, it rates high on the scale for diagnostic depth.

Strategically, the Triangle also rates high on the scale for offering specific strategic options in working with the three types of interests, options that flow directly from the diagnosis of the wants, needs, hopes, and fears of the party in conflict. The three strategies of

1. Focusing on Common Interests,
2. Working with the Three Types of Interests Differently, and
3. Moving the Parties Around the Triangle to Avoid Impasse

are clearly interrelated and work together well to help the parties get what they need as they move toward resolution.

Final Thoughts on the Triangle of Satisfaction

The Triangle is an elegant and simple model that can be used at many levels, both at the surface with just Result type interests, or much deeper through Process and Psychological interests. In fact, the Triangle is sometimes drawn in a slightly different way to illustrate this, as in the figure below:

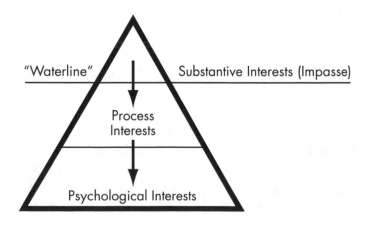

In this model, the Triangle is presented as an iceberg, with the tip of the iceberg, the part that is most obvious to us, being the Result or substantive interests. Below the surface, however, are a range of Process interests we need to take into account, and an even deeper layer of Psychological interests that we may need to address. If we simply work with what we see on the surface we are likely to suffer the same fate as the Titanic, by running aground on the parts of the problem that are not readily apparent but are there waiting to trip the unwary practitioner who has failed to properly diagnose the problem.

PRACTITIONER'S WORKSHEET FOR THE TRIANGLE OF SATISFACTION MODEL

1. Develop the full range of Interests for each party, and diagnose by type.

2. Focus on Common Interests, and explore Competing Interests by looking for additional Common Interests.

Party A's Interests:	Party B's Interests:
Result: • • • •	Result: • • • •
Process: • • • •	Process: • • • •

Party A's Interests:	Party B's Interests:
Psychological: • • • •	Psychological: • • • •
Common Interests: • • • •	• • • •

3. Work with the Three Types of Interests differently. Some specific interventions for each type of interest are:

Result Interests:
• Brainstorm ideas
• Jointly problem-solve
• Develop multiple options
• Exchange value, dovetail value
• Consider compromise
• Bargain if necessary

Process Interests:
• Continually negotiate the Process to meet the parties' interests
• Include new or different people to change the dynamic at the table
• Think outside the "content" issues of the problem
• Look for objective standards
• Ensure the process is transparent and fair

• Ensure the process is balanced and inclusive
• Keep a future (solution) focus, not a past (blame) focus

Psychological Interests:
• Don't try to "solve" or bargain people's feelings
• Don't minimize or dismiss ("Just the facts, ma'am . . .")
• Make as important as the other types of interests
• Listen, acknowledge, and validate the feelings
• Don't judge emotional interests; accept them and work through them
• Focus on the future to rebuild relationship issues
• Uncover, name, and discuss identity issues, and stay focused on the full range of interests

4. Move Parties Around the Triangle to Avoid Impasse

• Consider Process interventions for Results problems;
• Consider Result interventions for Psychological problems;
• Consider Process interventions for Psychological problems;
• Consider Psychological interventions for Process problems.

ADDITIONAL CASE STUDY: TRIANGLE OF SATISFACTION

Case Study: Acme Foods

The situation was a termination and claimed wrongful dismissal of a 20-year employee. Acme is a very large corporation, with both union and non-union staff, the latter mostly in management positions. Cathy had worked at Acme as a unionized staff member for 14 years, and had been in a supervisory role for five years. One year before, she had taken a year-long sabbatical as part of a company "4 for 5" program, which allowed staff to receive 80 percent of their income for four years while working full time, then taking a year off and receiving 80 percent of their income while off. As part of the 4 for 5 agreement, the company required Cathy to commit to staying at her job for 12 months after her return, or there could be tax consequences. Cathy was the sole breadwinner in her family.

Cathy returned from her sabbatical and was told a restructuring was under way. One month later, she was laid off (along with 12 others), and offered a package of 18 months' notice. She refused to accept this and sued for wrongful dismissal. Cathy at this time was 55 years old, and the company had a retirement policy called an "80 factor," which meant that when an employee's age and years of service added up to 80, he or she could retire with full retirement income and benefits. Cathy, at this time, added up to 75, which, when combined with the notice period of 1.5 years, took her to 76.5, only 3.5 years short of full retirement. She wanted to find a way to get to her full 80 factor, so she could in fact retire with full pension and benefits.

Cathy claimed that the 4 for 5 agreement required her to stay for a full year after returning, and the company was obliged to keep her for that year. That would add one year of service and a year to her age, putting her within 1.5 of the 80 factor. In addition, the 4 for 5 agreement required she have a mentor in the company to help her find a new position in the company if she were laid off during the sabbatical; the company had not given her this mentor. She claimed that there were jobs she could do in the company, and the mentor would have helped her find a job internally. Barring that, she claimed that notice, given how she was treated in being terminated, should be 30 months, adding an additional year to her total. She asked that the company put her on a leave without pay for 6 more months, which would take her to the 80 factor. Finally, she wanted the VP of Human Resources to look at her case, convinced that he would not approve of how she was being treated.

The company, on the other hand, did not want to even consider helping her get to the 80 factor. They were downsizing, they had a hiring freeze, and while they conceded that they hadn't followed the 4 for 5 agreement exactly, they were not obliged to keep her for a year or to find a new position for her. They said that even if they had appointed a mentor, no jobs were available so it was irrelevant. In the past, this company had a culture of "cradle to grave" entitlement for employees. Now, new management had set new rules that they felt were fair, but not as generous; they were very clear that the rules would not be bent for anyone, since they wanted the message sent that the rules were the rules for all. The VP of Human Resources was the sponsor of these new rules. Also, the company pension plan had just gone from surplus to deficit, so they didn't want to burden it further by helping employees draw from the pension plan years earlier than they were entitled to.

Triangle of Satisfaction Diagnosis and Worksheet: Acme Foods

Cathy's Interests:	Acme Food's Interests:
Result: • Get to 80 factor, and retire • Get most money in settlement	Result: • Pay proper, fair severance, and no more • Close the file • Specifically not get Cathy to 80 factor

(Continued)

Cathy's Interests:	Acme Food's Interests:
Process: • Be treated fairly • Company live up to their obligations under agreement • Have this settled soon, avoid litigation • Get money soon, bills were mounting • Avoid litigating with Acme, known to be vindictive in court	Process: • Avoid litigation if possible • Stick to the rules, no special deals • Send a message to other employees
Psychological: • Feel that her years of service were valued • Feel that she "got the most" • Feel that senior people (the VP) had reviewed her situation and knew what was going on	Psychological: • Show that employees are valued, but treated the same • Have Cathy understand there is nothing personal in their decisions • Let Cathy know senior people have reviewed the file • Help Cathy in any way reasonable
Common Interests: • Fair treatment • Value Cathy for years of service • Process for senior review of final deal • Avoid prolonged litigation	• Close the file, move on • Help Cathy as much as possible • Let her know that the VP had reviewed the situation

From a diagnosis point of view, each party had a full range of interests. In addition, while there was a strong set of competing interests (mostly centred around the Result or substantive interests), there were also a number of common interests.

Triangle of Satisfaction Strategic Direction: Acme Foods

Strategy #1 is to focus on common interests.

Common Interests Focus:	Possible Intervention Action:
Highlight for parties: Both want fair treatment in the final settlement.	• On the money side, since this is a lawsuit, look for objective standards for "fairness" in notice periods for employees. The lawyers can have a discussion focusing on this to get the parties into the same ballpark and away from the extreme positions taken.
Highlight for parties: Value and appreciate Cathy's years of service, and help Cathy as much as possible.	• Mediator could raise this issue, and have company representatives address this. In this case, the company reps had her file, and praised her for the quality of service to the organization and again explained it was not personal; it was Acme's drastically changing business needs that caused this. • Mediator could initiate discussion of other ways company could help Cathy, such as letters of reference, keep her high on the list for consideration if new positions come available, etc.

(Continued)

Common Interests Focus:	Possible Intervention Action:
Highlight for parties: Cathy's desire to have senior people review the situation, and Acme's desire for Cathy to know their offer meets new company guidelines authorized all the way up the chain of command.	• Parties discussed and agreed that company reps would call the Vice President during the mediation, so Cathy could satisfy herself that senior management backed up the policies being put forward at the table.
In caucus, highlight for parties: The desire to close the file and avoid prolonged litigation.	• Test Cathy's need to settle quickly and avoid litigation. • Test Acme's need to avoid a costly public display of fighting with a valued and respected employee, i.e., what message this would send to the employees staying.

Strategy #2 is to treat different types of interests differently.

Type of Interest:	Possible Intervention:
Substantive Interests:	• Explore objective criteria, such as typical notice period ranges. • Discuss the obligation of the company to get an employee to the 80 factor. • Discuss the way that the layoff was handled. • Inform Cathy who else was laid off (to see if it was personal or much broader than just Cathy). • Privately meet with just the lawyers to bargain the notice period.

Type of Interest:	Possible Intervention:
Substantive Interests:	• Explore the real consequences and costs of Cathy waiting an extra year or two to get to the 80 factor. • Explore other needs of Cathy, such as tax implications, letters of reference, benefits continuation, payment structure, etc.
Process Interests:	• In caucus, explore the costs of proceeding, and compare with what is on offer today. • Explore why Cathy feels unfairly treated, and look at ways of addressing that, both in monetary and non-monetary terms. • Explore with Acme other areas of flexibility that may be possible; look at what they could "sell" back at the office. • Explore any joint messages to other employees if they reached a settlement. • Put Cathy in touch with the VP, someone she has great respect for. • Meet separately with counsel for hard bargaining the dollars, sparing Cathy that process.
Psychological Interests:	• Explore Cathy and Acme rep's past relationship, as it may either help or reveal a deeper problem.

(Continued)

Type of Interest:	Possible Intervention:
Psychological Interests:	• Discuss Cathy's career at Acme, and let Acme reps personally recognize Cathy's contribution while there. • Let Cathy push as hard as she needs to, so that she can feel she "got the most" from the company. • Let Cathy talk with the Vice President, so she feels he takes her situation seriously (regardless of the final outcome).

Strategy #3 is to move around the Triangle to avoid impasse. In this case, it would mean moving between the interventions above, spending time at the beginning getting some recognition for Cathy's service first, then looking at non-monetary options to help Cathy, then bargaining the numbers for a while, then moving back to arranging a meeting with the Senior Vice President, then finalizing the numbers through bargaining, then looking at the proposed settlement and comparing it to prolonged litigation and those outcomes, etc. By moving around and between the different types of interests, it allows maximum movement in each area, and avoids getting stuck in any one of them.

Epilogue of the Case Study
In this case, Cathy fundamentally wanted to get to her 80 factor, and Acme fundamentally refused to make that a goal of theirs. This was headed for an impasse.

Instead, parties spent some time talking about the changes in the workplace and the new management team's change in culture and rules. The company rep indicated that the other 11 laid-off employees were treated the same, and while they didn't like it they had accepted it as fair. Acme told a story of one of the 11 who was only 10 months from his 80 factor, and the company, based on the new policy, would not "bridge" him to get him there. Therefore, out of fairness to all, they could not with Cathy. (This focused on Process—i.e., fairness—interests). In addition, the representatives knew Cathy and had worked with her; they acknowledged her years of service and high-quality work, making clear that this was painful and difficult for the company and for them, and most certainly wasn't personal. (This acknowledgment focused on the Psychological interests.)

Looking at possible resolutions, Acme pointed out they understood her position, and indicated that they would do this for Cathy. Acme had a choice to pay any notice period as a lump sum (which was easier for the company), or to keep Cathy on payroll for the notice period offered. The difference was that the notice period, if paid through payroll, counted toward her 80 factor, and would shorten the time it would take for her to start getting pension benefits. Plus, she would remain on the company benefits plan as opposed to getting cash in lieu, which was important since no individual can get the same quality of benefits plan on their own. If it didn't settle, however, they would only pay a lump sum, and it would be of less value to Cathy in terms of her goals.

The lawyers then discussed ranges of notice periods, and they narrowed the range to 20 to 26 months as fair and reasonable. When the offer came from Acme at 24 months, this was seen as acceptable. (This was a shift to substantive interests.) In addition, on the non-monetary side, Acme agreed to let Cathy know when new positions opened up (not giving her a right of refusal, just knowledge of the position), and Cathy saw this as a benefit.

Finally, Cathy asked to speak with the Senior Vice President. The Acme reps got him on the line, and Cathy spoke with him for a few minutes. He reiterated the significant change in culture that was taking place, apologized for laying her off, and hoped that it would resolve. It was clear to Cathy that this was the best offer she could get (Process and Psychological interests). The matter settled.

By understanding the different types of interests, and by following the Triangle from a strategic perspective, the practitioner helped the parties focus on meeting their interests in the most effective way possible.

— CHAPTER SIX —

MODEL #3:
THE BOUNDARY MODEL

BACKGROUND OF THE BOUNDARY MODEL

A model unlike the first two discussed so far is a model developed by conflict resolution practitioner Larry Prevost.[1] In his doctoral dissertation, Prevost looked at the nature of conflict and crisis, and suggested an underlying framework to understand what drove conflict. The Boundary model is a creative and unique way of looking at conflict that attempts to frame conflict through a single, specific lens.

DIAGNOSIS WITH THE BOUNDARY MODEL

The Boundary model suggests that the common element that all things, people and organisms share is "boundaries." Boundaries operate on many levels. On a physical level, everything has a physical boundary and physical limits. On a behavioural level, all activity is subject to boundaries of many kinds. Boundaries in human society take the form of laws, agreements, contracts, rules, procedures, conventions, orders, decisions, and so on.

1. Dr. Larry Prevost is a practitioner in the field, and developed this model as part of his dissertation for his Ph.D. in Philosophy, "The Core Elements of Reality," LaSalle University, 1996.

Boundaries, as the model defines them, have four key elements:

1. **Defined Standards for Behaviour:** Boundaries must have defined standards for maximum and/or minimum allowable behaviour. These standards are a form of limits that the boundary establishes. For example, on our highways the speed limit typically defines a maximum speed of 100 kph, and a minimum speed (typically in the 60 or 70 kph range). If you exceed the limits in either direction, you are subject to a fine.

2. **Jurisdiction or Legitimacy:** Boundaries must have "jurisdiction," which is a source of legitimacy for existing at all. In our highway example, that legitimacy comes from the Highway Traffic Act as passed by the province or the state, or from one of the many related laws that our government has jurisdiction to enact to control the roads and highways.

3. **Authority or Enforcement:** Boundaries must have some form of "authority." Authority in this case is an entity, process, or person(s) responsible for enforcing the boundary. Without any process or person(s) enforcing a limit, the boundary effectively doesn't exist. In the highway example, the police are the authority for enforcing the Highway Traffic Act.

4. **Norms:** Boundaries usually (though not always) have a certain degree of tolerance or latitude or variance, which are called "norms." Norms are the reasonable latitudes around the boundary that we accept without perceiving the boundary to have been violated. In our highway example, if you asked the average driver how fast you could go on the highway without risking a ticket, the minimum you are likely to hear is 110 kph. This means that although the *boundary* is 100 kph, the *norm* is actually 110 kph.

Boundary Model

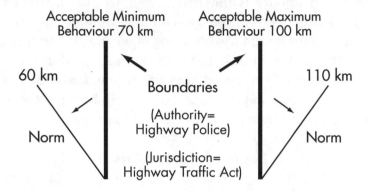

There are two key definitions that the practitioner needs for working with conflict in the Boundary model. They are:

- **Definition of "Conflict" in the Boundary Model:** Conflict is caused when a boundary and its norms are challenged, threatened, or circumvented. Conflict requires an intervention in order to resolve it. If the norm, for example, expands to 120 kph, and the party with jurisdiction or authority for this boundary fails to intervene, it starts to threaten the existence of the boundary.

Boundary Model: Conflict

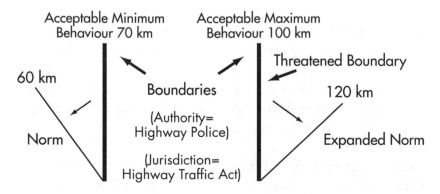

• **Definition of "Crisis":** A crisis is an escalation of the conflict. When a boundary is threatened, violated, or circumvented, and this situation is allowed to continue without intervention, it results in the boundary collapsing altogether. When this happens, it causes a crisis. If 120 kph routinely goes unpunished, there is effectively no speed limit left on the roads resulting in the norm continuing to expand at will. In the end, there will be a significant increase in accidents and deaths.

Boundary Model: Crisis

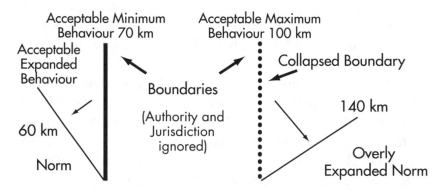

The Boundary model states that most conflict is caused by four specific reasons directly related to how people interact with the boundaries they face:

A lack of clarity around what the boundary is. For example, a new employee may not know that breaks are strictly timed and enforced in this workplace. The employee may be told to "go grab a coffee and a smoke," and then get yelled at when he returns 30 minutes later. Boundaries must be clear and specific for them to be enforceable.

Lack of acceptance of who has authority to enforce a boundary. For example, an employee approaches a colleague about taking too long on his break, only to have the other employee respond, "It's not your job to be watching my breaks." Essentially, the colleague is refusing to accept the authority of a co-worker. In a family, a child may say, "But Mom said I could," implying that Dad has no authority over what Mom decides.

Lack of acceptance of who has jurisdiction over a boundary. For example, a company refuses to comply with an "industry-led" voluntary initiative to reduce emissions, saying that no law requires them to comply. This is a way of refuting the jurisdiction of the industry at large to hold them to a boundary.

A deliberate expansion of a boundary past acceptable norms. For example, an employee comes in a few days about five minutes late. No one says anything, as others in the office do this once in a while. Soon, the employee is coming in 15 minutes late frequently. Management says nothing, but other employees start to complain (conflict). Not long after, the employee is regularly 20 to 30 minutes late, and on occasion 45 minutes late. Other employees now start doing the same, and when a memo is issued asking all staff to be on time, it is largely ignored (crisis). In this example, the norms began to expand with no intervention. When norms are sufficiently expanded, conflict and crisis ensues.

According to the model, the most common causes of conflict are a lack of clarity about boundaries and norms, or a deliberate "pushing of the envelope" to expand the norms as far as possible, reasons #1 and #4 above. It is human nature to push boundaries and expand norms. Children are constantly testing the boundaries we set, often to find out what will happen if they either expand them or violate them. While it may appear that this tendency to "push the envelope" is the cause of much conflict, the real cause is that the people with jurisdiction and authority often overlook the expanded norms. It's this lack of intervention that sustains and escalates the conflict.

CASE STUDY: BOUNDARY MODEL DIAGNOSIS

For the purposes of our Case Study, we'll diagnose three boundary issues (and identify a fourth) that appear to be a source of conflict between these three people. While there are others, we shall focus on these three to demonstrate how the model works.

To start with, there are two broad boundaries that exist in almost all workplaces:

1. management's right to make operational decisions that employees must abide by, and

2. the workers' right to a safe workplace, free of harassment and discrimination.

Keeping these general boundaries in mind, three areas of boundary conflict in the Case Study are:

- **Start and finish times of the job (Deliberate expansion of norms):**
  Clearly, the established start-time boundary is 9:00 am, and Bob is violating this boundary. He states that "others do this as well," implying that he is behaving within the "norm," a view not shared by Sally. For Sally, the norm is that staff can be 10 to 20 minutes late a few times per year, whereas Bob feels that the norm allows weekly attendance at work this late.

- **Legitimate chain of command followed (Challenging the jurisdiction and authority):**
  In this case, Sally has established a new requirement or boundary that Bob take direction from Diane. Bob appears

to be refusing to accept this decision and is thereby violating this boundary. A refusal to follow direction from the person you report to is often referred to as insubordination. Bob, however, does not view Sally's judgment or decision as legitimate, and therefore is challenging both her jurisdiction and authority in the situation. After being threatened with discipline, Bob adopts a "work-to-rule" approach, a strategy that tacitly acknowledges Sally's authority (Bob wouldn't have changed anything if he felt Sally had no authority at all) while at the same time refutes Sally's jurisdiction or right to require him to take direction from Diane.

- **Respectful behaviour in the workplace (Lack of clarity of the boundary around respect, or deliberately expanding the norms):**
  This boundary issue relates to the way Diane speaks to Bob; Bob believes that Diane is violating a boundary that requires respect in the workplace. Most workplaces have boundaries around respectful behaviour, though few are clearly articulated. Bob feels that Diane is violating this boundary; Diane clearly doesn't feel she is being all that disrespectful, especially given how she feels Bob is behaving.

A fourth boundary issue exists between Sally and the union, with the union claiming that she is breaching the collective agreement by assigning tasks not related to the worker's job classification, something the collective agreement doesn't allow. That boundary issue appears headed for arbitration where unresolved collective agreement boundary disputes are resolved.

In all three situations described above, the parties are solidly in conflict, meaning that the boundaries between the parties appear to have been violated, and/or the jurisdiction and authority of the boundary is being challenged. Unless an intervention takes place, it will quickly develop into a crisis and begin spreading to other employees in the area.

As we can see, diagnosing the situation through the Boundary model often yields very behavioural results, meaning that Boundary model analysis tends to be functional and practical, rather than psychological or theoretical. Let's look now at what the Boundary model can suggest in terms of interventions that may help.

STRATEGIC DIRECTION FROM THE BOUNDARY MODEL

Strategically, the model suggests that when a conflict or crisis occurs, there must be an intervention. This intervention must have as its primary goal the re-establishment of all four elements of the boundary.

1. **Boundary Clarified and Re-established:** The first step must be to re-establish the boundary itself, not the norms. Norms are defined as the reasonable or accepted latitude to the boundary, and have no formal existence in and of themselves. For example, if you receive a speeding ticket for going 140 kph in a 100 kph zone, the ticket is for 40 kph over the speed limit; the court does not say, "Well, since traveling at 110 kph is the norm, you were really only speeding by 30 kph." The boundary itself is what has legitimacy, and that is what must be re-established.

2. **Jurisdiction Clarified and Re-established:** The jurisdiction must be established and accepted by all parties. Until all parties accept the legitimacy of whoever is establishing the rules, those rules will not be respected.

3. **Authority Clarified and Re-established:** The authority must be established and accepted by all parties. Until all

parties accept the authority of whoever is monitoring and maintaining the rules, those rules will not be respected.

4. **Norms Allowed**: Finally, as an optional step and only after the above three steps have been taken, some reasonable latitude from the boundary may be allowed. It's an optional step because a "zero tolerance" policy may also be appropriate, which simply means that the norm becomes identical to the boundary. Should certain norms be allowed, they must be monitored closely, as there is a strong human tendency to continually expand the norms whenever possible.

Based on the interventions that the Boundary model suggests, a simple guide can be developed based on the diagnosis of what is causing the conflict:

Diagnosis:	Strategic Intervention:
Violation of a boundary due to lack of clarity or differing expectations:	Clarify the boundary; discuss the expectations of all parties. Clarify the consequences of boundary violation.
Violation of the boundary due to deliberate expansion of its norms:	Re-establish and clarify the boundary.
Lack of acceptance of jurisdiction:	Gain acceptance of the jurisdiction; re-establish legitimacy for the jurisdiction. Bring in higher authority to clarify and define jurisdiction if needed. Negotiate new jurisdiction if appropriate.

(Continued)

Diagnosis:	Strategic Intervention:
Lack of acceptance of authority:	Gain acceptance of who has authority; re-establish legitimacy for authority. Bring in higher authority to clarify and define authority issues if needed. Enforce boundary if necessary. Negotiate new levels of authority if appropriate.

Based on the above strategic interventions, let's look at what the parties in the Case Study might do to manage the conflict.

CASE STUDY: BOUNDARY MODEL STRATEGIC DIRECTION

In the Case Study, the strategies to intervene can be applied to all three issues identified in the diagnosis.

Start and Finish Times Followed

Clearly, the established start time is 9:00 am, and Bob is violating this boundary. The only question is whether he is within the workplace norms. Assuming Sally as the "practitioner" in this situation (in other words, there is no mediator or third party helping; Sally is assuming responsibility to manage the conflict), she could intervene by re-establishing the start-time boundary and the expectation with Bob that he arrive no later than 9:00 am every day. Both Bob and Sally need to be clear what the consequences are, and Sally, as the authority, needs to enforce the boundary if it is violated again. In addition, Sally can explore with Bob the reasons Bob has been late, and look at other solutions, such as flex time, to see if that might solve the problem for both parties. The key step here, however, is to re-establish and clarify the boundary. In response to Bob's statement that "Others are doing it," Sally should ensure that the other team members are held equally accountable for understanding and complying with the start and finish time boundary.

Legitimate Chain of Command Followed

In this case, Sally has established a new boundary or requirement that Bob take direction from Diane. Bob, however, does not view Sally's judgment or decision as legitimate, and therefore is challenging both her jurisdiction and authority in the situation. Sally needs to explore Bob's reasons for rejecting her jurisdiction, and what he would need to willingly accept her authority. By focusing on the future, the practitioner (Sally) can help find a way to either re-establish acceptance of the jurisdiction and authority voluntarily, or mandate it through either discipline or a higher authority becoming involved. Either way, the model guides the practitioner to help re-establish the legitimacy of the jurisdiction and authority between them. In the case of a "work-to-rule" approach, the difficulty lies in the fact that the worker is technically operating within the boundary, although at its absolute minimum. In other words, the authority is being acknowledged, but the jurisdiction is implicitly being challenged. The task here for the practitioner is to explore what Bob needs[2] to fully accept the jurisdiction involved and get back to "normal" performance.

Respectful Behaviour in the Workplace

Most workplaces have boundaries around respectful behaviour, though few are clearly articulated. The practitioner needs to help the parties explore what a reasonable boundary around respectful behaviour is, how both would define it and monitor it, and help them agree to implement a new (and clearer) boundary around this issue. To accomplish this, Sally needs to help Diane understand the company harassment policy and ensure that her behaviour doesn't breach the policy.

2. The practitioner should consider the Triangle model to help with assessing and working with Bob's interests.

Sally could also speak to Bob to find out what he wanted to accomplish from the harassment complaint, and how else they may be able to meet that.

ASSESSING AND APPLYING THE BOUNDARY MODEL

Diagnostically, this model is reasonably deep, meaning it can help diagnose potential causes of conflict in a variety of circumstances. That said, it also restricts its diagnosis to boundary-related issues, meaning that it is limited in the range or scope of diagnosis. That puts this model at medium on the diagnostic scale.

Strategically, it offers clear ideas for intervention, along with key goals for the intervention that can guide a practitioner. It rates high on the strategic side of the model.

While the Boundary model is extremely useful in a wide range of conflicts, it probably has its greatest usefulness in relational conflict, conflict in which the parties will continue to interact after the dispute is resolved. An assessment of boundary issues along with a focus on better clarity around boundaries carries an implicit assumption that future interactions are likely. In situations where no future interactions are likely, Boundary analysis becomes more abstract and less functional or practical for the practitioner.

PRACTITIONER'S WORKSHEET FOR THE BOUNDARY MODEL

1. Identify the issues in the conflict, and for each one, identify the boundary that is violated, circumvented, or threatened.

Conflict Issues:	Boundary Violated:

2. Intervene based on the diagnosis above:

Diagnosis:	Strategic Intervention:
Violation of a boundary due to lack of clarity or differing expectations:	Clarify the boundary; discuss the expectations of all parties. Clarify the consequences of boundary violation.
Violation of the boundary due to deliberate expansion of its norms:	Re-establish and clarify the boundary.
Lack of acceptance of jurisdiction:	Gain acceptance of the jurisdiction; re-establish legitimacy for the jurisdiction. Bring in higher authority to clarify and define jurisdiction if needed. Negotiate new jurisdiction if appropriate.
Lack of acceptance of authority:	Gain acceptance of who has authority; re-establish legitimacy for authority. Bring in higher authority to clarify and define authority issues if needed. Enforce boundary if necessary. Negotiate new levels of authority if appropriate.

ADDITIONAL CASE STUDY: BOUNDARY MODEL

Case Study: Mutiny at the Office

The situation involved a small work team, eight staff and a new manager. The new manager was a former colleague of about half the team, though not in the past few years. The new manager was brought in to replace the manager who had retired, and who was very well liked.

About six months after taking over the role of manager, the team effectively mutinied. They refused to work for the new manager, telling the director that this manager had imposed new rules on them, ignored their knowledge and ability to do the job, treated them like children, and didn't listen to any of their concerns or complaints. They refused to take assignments that they didn't want, that didn't make sense to them, and that were different from before. The team believed that the new manager was incompetent and shouldn't even be a manager. The team as a whole wanted this appointee to be reassigned and a new manager, ideally someone from the team of eight, appointed.

The manager saw the situation very differently, believing that the departing manager had been popular mainly because he didn't manage the team and let them get away with whatever they wanted to. Work efficiency was low, there was conflict on the team over jobs and roles, and there were even some anonymous complaints that people left early or came in late and nothing was done about it. What the new manager had done, in his own view, was to simply enforce the rules of the workplace the way they were written.

A mediator was brought in and everyone was interviewed. It became clear that to a large degree both parties were right. The new manager was behaving rigidly and didn't spend much time listening to the team members. He was intent on "whipping the team into shape." In doing so, he had lost the

respect of the team. The team was clearly used to doing whatever it wanted, as the past manager had let the team handle
work assignments and job duties on their own, rarely getting
involved unless all heck had broken loose. The team was used
to making a lot of their own decisions, frequently ending up
with solutions that were inefficient but that catered to the
desires of one or two of the more senior team members.

Boundary Model Diagnosis and Worksheet: Mutiny at the Office

1. Identify the Issues in the conflict, and for each one, identify
   the boundary that is violated or threatened.

Conflict Issues:	Boundary Violated:
Refusing to take work assigned by the manager.	Management has a right to assign work, and providing it is safe and reasonable, it must be done. In this case, the team refused the jurisdiction and authority of the new manager.
Manager not listening to team concerns.	There is an implicit boundary that everyone, staff included, has a right to be heard if they have concerns. The manager violated the team's expectations by refusing to listen.

Conflict Issues:	Boundary Violated:
Past practices dramatically changed.	The previous manager had a completely different set of boundaries and workplace rules, which this new manager changed unilaterally and without consultation or reasoning to the team, other than, "He was wrong, I'm right." Since this was not acceptable to the team, they simply rejected this manager's jurisdiction and authority to make those changes.
Start and finish times.	The workday has specific boundaries around the workday, and these were not being respected. Norms were expanded well past the boundary.

Boundary Model Strategic Direction: Mutiny at the Office

2. Based on the above diagnosis, the following interventions should be considered.

Diagnosis:	Strategic Intervention Options:
Lack of acceptance of jurisdiction and/or authority: The team, in essence, refused to take work assignments from this manager.	Bring the director in to speak with the team, and clarify: This manager has both the right and the full authority of the organization to make changes. In fact, this manager was chosen by the director specifically to make major changes and improve the efficiency of this team.
Lack of acceptance of jurisdiction and/or authority: The team rejected this manager's legitimacy as a manager.	The team needs to accept the manager's role, jurisdiction, and authority. To accomplish this, the team has to detail what it reasonably needs from the manager to be comfortable in accepting the manager as their leader.
Violation of a boundary due to lack of clarity or differing expectations: Manager not listening to the team, not explaining the reasoning or the direction the team is going in.	The boundary around the team being listened to, being included in some decision-making, or explanation of decisions had to be re-established. A process for getting time with the manager had to be agreed upon, along with a process for communicating the new vision and direction the new manager is taking the team in.

Diagnosis:	Strategic Intervention Options:
Violation of a boundary due to lack of clarity or differing expectations: Start and finish times re-established.	Management must clarify the boundary around start and finish times, along with the exceptions to this that are acceptable (sickness, etc.). This boundary must be reset, and the norms brought back to the boundary.

The mediator followed a number of the above interventions, including:

• A team meeting with the director, who laid out the mandate this manager had been given, along with clarifying that the previous manager's practices were not acceptable. This helped reset some of the expectations of the team.

• A full team meeting to explore the questions:
   - What changes need to be made by the manager for the team to fully accept him as leader?
   - What changes need to be made by the team for the manager to feel supported and accepted?

This was at times quite difficult for the manager, as he had to make important changes to his style of leadership. For example, he typically offered little access to his team on a daily basis. To have a meeting with him, team members often had to book time more than a week in advance. As part of the changes, he had to make time on the same day if a team member requested it. In addition, he had to work hard on his listening skills, and move away from simply telling the team why he was right and they were wrong.

The team also had to make changes, agreeing to raise issues directly with the manager rather than complaining amongst the team.

Epilogue of the Case Study

All boundary work was documented in the form of a "Team Charter," and after three sessions was agreed to by the team as a whole. This outlined the principles and definitions of all the boundary issues that needed changing. The team then requested two months to pilot the changes and see how they worked.

After two months, seven of the eight staff members were both content and pleased with the changes on the team, with one exception: the eighth team member. She refused to accept the Team Charter and continued calling for the manager to be moved or fired. She constantly raised issues about the manager with her peers and refused to deal directly with the manager on those issues as had been agreed by the team as a whole. In the final team meeting, the other seven team members, citing the changes the manager had made, told this worker that the problem now was her, not the manager. The eighth team member walked out of the room.

In a separate session, this team member indicated that the manager used to be a personal friend (with some indication that they might have been romantically involved or attracted), but they had had a major falling-out. She indicated that she could not under any circumstances accept that manager as her boss. In other words, she would never accept the authority and jurisdiction of this person regardless of the changes the manager might make.

After discussions with senior management, it was decided by everyone (including the employee and the union) that she would be transferred to a different position under another manager.

— CHAPTER SEVEN —

MODEL #4:
INTERESTS, RIGHTS, AND POWER

BACKGROUND OF THE
INTERESTS/RIGHTS/POWER MODEL

This model is a foundational framework used in the conflict resolution field. In many ways, it underpins the entire field of conflict resolution and negotiation. Two of the main sources for this model are the original works of Fisher and Ury at the Project on Negotiation at Harvard, specifically in their books *Getting to Yes*[1] and *Getting Past No*.[2] In addition, many authors and researchers in the field have worked extensively with the three concepts in the model and how they interrelate in the context of Conflict Systems Design. These concepts, however, tend to be used fairly loosely and without enough cohesion to form a "model" in the way we are using this term. This book takes the next step by arranging and structuring the Interests/Rights/Power (I/R/P) model into a functional format.

Diagnosis with the I/R/P Model

Diagnostically, this model focuses on the many processes and approaches to resolving disputes that people use, rather than

1. Roger Fisher, William Ury, and Bruce Patton, *Getting to Yes: Negotiating Agreement Without Giving In* (New York: Penguin Books, 1991).
2. William Ury, *Getting Past No: Negotiating Your Way From Confrontation to Collaboration* (New York: Bantam Books, 1991).

categorizing or assessing the conflicts themselves. This model identifies the three basic categories or types of processes that are used to resolve conflict, and states that all dispute resolution approaches people use fall into one of these three categories:

Interest-based Processes

This is an approach that tries to reconcile or find a solution that meets the interests of the parties. Interests refer to the parties' wants, needs, hopes, and fears. Interest-based approaches are or tend to be more consensual, and succeed when both parties get enough of their interests met to agree on a solution.
Type of Outcome: Win/Win
Process Examples: Most types of negotiation, mediation, joint problem solving, mutual gains bargaining, brainstorming

Rights-based Processes

This is an approach that is characterized by parties asserting or focusing on the superiority of one party's rights over the rights of the other parties. Rights come from many sources, including laws, statutes, conventions, past practices, policies, contracts, etc. Rights-based processes tend to be adversarial, and focus on promoting one's own rights while minimizing and de-legitimizing the other parties' rights.
Type of Outcome: Win/Lose
Process Examples: Litigation, arbitration, adjudication, tribunal decision, neutral evaluation, some types of negotiation, formal investigation

Power-based Processes

This approach is characterized by parties bringing to bear all the resources they have at their disposal against the other party in an attempt to win. Typically, power-based processes are highly adversarial, and are sometimes applied in spite of the rights of the parties.

Type of Outcome: Lose/Lose (although sometimes Win/Lose)
Process Examples: Threats, intimidation, physical force or violence, strikes or lockouts, unilateral decision-making, some types of negotiation, "self-help," and voting

It should be noted that rights- and power-based processes, while separate and distinguishable types of processes, often operate together in conflict because it's often the rights-based framework that gives power to a party in the situation. For example, many governments have created rights-based laws which grant police the power to arrest and incarcerate individuals. In addition, rights- and power-based processes share some traits in that both are adversarial in nature, whereas interest-based processes are collaborative in nature.

The simplest format for the Interests/Rights/Power (I/R/P) model is the Stairway Model:

Interests/Rights/Power Model: Diagnosis

DISPUTE RESOLUTION STAIRWAY

POWER

RIGHTS

INTERESTS

Control Goes Down

Costs Go Up

The stairway model indicates that as parties move up the stairway with the type of process they are using to resolve a conflict, two things happen:

1. **The costs go up.** Costs, in relation to conflict, are an important consideration. The most obvious costs of conflict are time and money, but when dealing with conflict, a whole

additional range of costs will surface. Some of these other costs are incurred as the conflict moves up the stairway:

- Loss of productivity
- Loss of focus
- Draining of emotional energy
- Stress
- Strained or terminated relationships
- Loss of productivity
- Lower morale
- Damaged reputation
- More time spent on the conflict
- More money and other resources spent on the conflict

Consider the full range of costs when comparing a few days negotiating a resolution to a contract dispute or an employment matter, to taking the same matter to litigation or a human rights tribunal that could run months or years. The full range of costs goes up dramatically when engaging in a rights-based process. Compare that, finally, to the same contract or employment dispute that escalates to power, where one party to a failed contract tries to destroy the reputation of another party in the community, or engages in theft or sabotage against their employer because of a dispute. Costs can go up even further.

2. **Control goes down**. When using interest-based processes, the parties themselves control the nature, direction, and outcome of the negotiations. When the process escalates to rights-based processes, the parties have turned the final decision over to a third party, whether a judge, an arbitrator, or a tribunal. And since rights-based processes typically only rule on the rights-based aspects of the dispute, many times the final decision handed down does not meet all of

the interests of either party, including the "winning" party. This is the case when *both* parties to a lawsuit appeal the judge's decision. When the dispute turns to power-based processes, the only control left each party is control over how much of their power they choose to use against the other party. In many situations where power is used against the other party, it often results in rapid escalation in a "tit-for-tat" exchange, leaving both parties feeling that they have no choice but to respond in kind. The situation rapidly spirals out of the control of both parties.

The assessment that the practitioner makes about what kind of process or processes the parties are using becomes a critical one when looking at the dynamics of the processes involved. The type of process being used, in other words, will greatly influence the outcomes the parties get.

It is important to note that the model in no way judges the use of rights- or power-based processes as being negative or wrong. The model simply notes that rights- and power-based processes are more costly (see the list of costs on the previous page) than interest-based approaches. Below is some detail on the strengths and weaknesses of each approach:

Strengths and Weaknesses of Interests, Rights, and Power Processes

Strengths:	Weaknesses:
Interest-based Process:	**Interest-based Process:**
• Collaborative	• Time-consuming
• Creative, unique solutions	• More creative but less consistent solutions
• Problem-solving approach	
• Durable agreements	• Doesn't always achieve a resolution
• Builds and strengthens relationships	• Can be (incorrectly) seen as a "soft" or "touchy-feely" approach
• Maximizes outcome for all parties	

(Continued)

Strengths:	Weaknesses:
Rights-based Process: • Fair, consistent standard applied to everyone • Faster outcomes, in that the solution to most situations is already spelled out • Rights-based positions have some external legitimacy • Can be seen as "objective"	**Rights-based Process:** • Win/lose outcome • More formal, costlier processes • Hard to get agreement on interpreting everyone's rights, and thus leads to additional conflict • Less flexible • People less satisfied when losing • Can harm relationships • Slower outcomes, since formal processes take longer than informal ones.
Power-based Process: • Fast, no consultation is required • One party can simply take everything they want (if, indeed, they can)	**Power-based Process:** • Can be seen as oppressive, stirs up resistance • Win/lose at best, often lose/lose • Significant damage to relationships • No durability to solutions, other party looking for failure or "I told you so!" • Once power is primary process used, more and more power is needed over time to get the same result • Never feels fair to the "losing" party (or often to either party)

CASE STUDY: I/R/P DIAGNOSIS

Applying the I/R/P model to our Case Study can give the practitioner clear insight into the type of processes the parties are using, the dynamics of the conflict in light of this, and why the parties are behaving the way they are.

In our Case Study, the problems started when Sally announced, in her role as the manager, that there would be changes made to the workflows and service levels, and as part of that there would be the creation of the AS-1 position. She announced this as a done deal. In other words, the initiation of the entire problem began when Sally started by approaching the implementation of a significant change in the workplace on the basis of her **power** or authority.

The next step, the job competition, is essentially a **rights-based** process, in that the collective agreement gives everyone the right to apply for open positions and prescribes a structured process that must meet certain criteria to be deemed fair. Since **rights-based** processes are essentially win/lose, Bob was angry when he lost, and felt he had no choice but to appeal the process, using yet another **rights-based** process (the appeal process).

Sally and the union met, and when the union raised their concerns about the fairness of the process, both parties agreed to rerun the competition using criteria that were mutually agreeable. This is the first and only use of an **interest-based** process, but it was an interest-based process that did not take Bob's interests into account, only the union's and management's.

After losing the second competition Bob attempted more **rights-based** appeals and grievances, none of which were successful. Bob then resorted to the only thing he felt he had left, a **power-based** process he alone controlled—his behaviour at work. He became difficult and resistant, adopting a "work-to-rule" approach to try and make the workplace unpleasant enough that they would give him what he wanted. Diane, in response, resorted to yelling and swearing to try to intimidate Bob into behaving better (**power-based**), which failed. Diane finally went to Sally, who would hopefully use her authority (**power-based**) to deal with Bob. Bob then initiated a harassment complaint to deal with Diane (**rights-based**).

As we can see, a large reason for the negative outcomes achieved by Sally, Bob, and Diane is that virtually every process they used fell into the rights and power category. Most of Sally, Diane, and Bob's behaviour became adversarial and costly in terms of time and energy; it damaged morale, productivity, and relationships in the workplace. These are all the classic costs of conflict the parties experience when escalating up the stairway.

What can a practitioner do after diagnosing the situation using the I/R/P model? Moving to the strategic use of the I/R/P model, we can look at some ideas for intervention that the model gives us.

STRATEGIC DIRECTION FROM THE I/R/P MODEL
The I/R/P model guides practitioners with the following strategies:

Default to Using Interest-based Processes First
There are very few situations where rights or power should be used as a first choice.[3] Interest-based processes such as problem-solving, negotiation, and mediation are inexpensive enough and successful enough that there should be a presumption of using these interest-based processes first. In other words, the default approach should be interest-based, moving to rights-based only if the interest-based fails, and moving to power-based only if the rights-based approach fails.

Use the Lowest-cost Rights or Power Process
Within each step, there are processes that will cost more or cost less. For example, arbitration typically costs less in time and

---

3. It is appropriate to default to Power first in emergency situations. At the scene of a fire or during an armed conflict, giving firefighters or soldiers orders that they follow immediately and without negotiation is an appropriate first approach. These situations, however, are rare.

money than litigation, even though both are rights-based processes. Even better, neutral evaluation costs less in time and money than either. In power-based processes, allowing people to vote for their political leaders every five years costs less than having a civil war every five years.

Loop Back to Interests

If you need to use rights- and/or power-based processes, or if the situation has escalated to other parties using rights- or power-based processes, look for opportunities to loop back down the stairway to interests wherever possible.

I/R/P Model: Strategic Direction

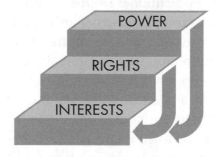

This is a key principle, and it says that if you need to file a lawsuit to protect your rights, do so; then keep looking for opportunities to negotiate a resolution. If you ground your son for breaking a curfew, look for ways in the future to negotiate a solution that works better for both of you; willing commitment is far better in most cases than imposed punishment. The concept of looping back is an important one, and one that we don't often think about when in the midst of conflict. Often, we are more focused on how we consolidate our power and escalate the conflict in an effort to win. This rarely succeeds or meets our interests without incurring significant costs to us along the way.

By understanding the outcomes and consequences of the different types of processes, this model directs practitioners to guide the parties toward the process that will accomplish what they want at the lowest cost for those involved.

CASE STUDY: I/R/P STRATEGIC DIRECTION

In continuing with the Case Study, we can look at what direction the I/R/P model would give in guiding the mediator's intervention. Below are four examples of the I/R/P strategies applied to Sally, Bob, and Diane.

Default to Using Interest-based Processes First

Since the first strategy is to default to interest-based processes, Sally (again as the practitioner in this example) could sit down with Bob to understand and discuss both of their interests. This exchange would avoid, for the moment, the power-based issues of insubordination or the rights-based issues of grievances, and focus on what Bob and Sally both want. To best help the two of them identify interests, the practitioner could review Model #2 "The Triangle of Satisfaction," and work with the common interests listed there. While there are a number of competing interests, there is also a full range of common interests for the parties to work with at this level. Sally could take the same approach with Bob regarding the harassment complaint, looking at what Bob really wants and how they might resolve it with Diane consensually.

Only Go to Rights if Interest-based Processes Fail

If one party is determined to focus on their own demands to the exclusion of the other party, the practitioner can focus for a while on the rights of the parties in the situation. For example, if Bob is adamant that he has a "right" to the promotion, Sally can help Bob explore those rights from the relative safety of this interest-based process of negotiation. Sally can explore how

Bob is viewing his rights, why the job competition process exists, why the union feels the process is fair, what rights Sally and Diane have, what basis he has for saying he has more rights than Diane or the union in this situation, etc. This is a low-cost way of exploring parties' rights, and much lower cost than constantly re-filing grievances or other complaints.[4]

Only Go to Power if Rights-based Processes Fail

Further, the practitioner could explore with Bob[5] what power he has in the situation, and what power the other party has. For example, the practitioner could use the idea of BATNA (Best Alternative to a Negotiated Agreement) and explore Bob's outcomes if he stays on power (the right to grieve, which the union has made clear has no merit, or work refusal and poor performance, which may result in dismissal), or if the status quo remains with no one getting what they want.

Loop Back to Interests

Finally, the practitioner can help Bob loop back to interests by helping Bob compare his rights and power options to what can be accomplished collaboratively—i.e., focusing on what he wants in the future and how Sally can help him, and what Sally wants and how he can help Sally. In this way, the parties can truly assess what they can accomplish jointly on an interest-based level and compare that to what an adversarial contest of their rights and their power looks like.

ASSESSING AND APPLYING THE I/R/P MODEL

Diagnostically, this model is basic and simple but at the same time very broad and applicable, because it can diagnose almost all dispute resolution processes as falling into one of the three categories. For this reason, it rates high on the diagnostic scale.

Strategically, it gives some direction (start with interests rather than rights or power; look for opportunities to loop back

---

4. This is a variation on Reality Testing or BATNA, i.e., looking at what a rights-based alternative looks like compared to the interest-based possibilities.
5. If the process is mediation and a third-party neutral is present, some of these strategies are better used in caucus than plenary. If the context is negotiation, as here in our example, exploring power-based processes or BATNAs is more sensitive, but can still be done.

to interests, etc.), but the strategic direction given by this model is fairly broad. Of more value strategically is understanding the win/win dynamic that interest-based processes can offer, contrasted with the win/lose and lose/lose dynamic of rights- and power-based processes. Overall it rates medium to medium-high on the depth of the strategic direction that it gives.

Final Thoughts on the I/R/P Model

The Interests/Rights/Power model is a foundational and seminal model in the conflict resolution field. It frames virtually every type of process that parties use to resolve or address conflict, and does so in a straightforward and elegant way. It is also a model that is both simple enough and useful enough that it can be taught to parties during the negotiation process itself to help everyone frame the choices that they're making, along with the dynamics or outcomes that may flow from those choices.

PRACTITIONER'S WORKSHEET FOR THE I/R/P MODEL

1. Assess the type of processes used so far by the parties, and the outcomes that they've been getting.

Interest-Based Processes Used:	Outcomes:
•	•
•	•
•	•
•	•
Rights-Based Processes Used:	Outcomes:
•	•
•	•
•	•
•	•

Power-Based Processes Used:	Outcomes:
•	•
•	•
•	•
•	•

2. Develop options for Interest-based processes that may help the parties:

_____

_____

_____

_____

_____

3. Identify low-cost Rights-based processes the parties should consider if Interest-based approaches fail:

_____

_____

_____

_____

_____

4. Identify low-cost Power-based processes the parties should consider if Rights-based processes should fail:

_____

_____

_____

_____

_____

5. Identify opportunities to loop back:

_____

_____

_____

_____

ADDITIONAL CASE STUDY – I/R/P MODEL

Case Study: The Greek Social Club

A tenant moved into an apartment next to a Greek social club that had been there for a number of years. The social club catered to the Greek community and held numerous functions at the club, mostly on weekends but sometimes on weekday nights.

Not long after moving in, the tenant went to the club during a party on a Friday night to talk to the manager about the noise. It was just after 10:00 pm. The manager listened to the tenant's complaint, but told him that the party would continue because the city's noise bylaw allowed them to make noise until 1:00 am on weekends. The tenant tried to explain that he worked shifts, and asked if the music could be turned down. Again, the manager refused, quoting the bylaw. The tenant left angry and immediately phoned the police. The police arrived at his apartment about half an hour later, listened to the story, and told him that the bylaw was indeed until 1:00 am, but they would talk to the club manager anyway. When the police showed up, the manager got extremely angry that the police had been called, and after the police left, he turned the music volume up. The tenant again called police, who visited once more but could do nothing.

Over the next few months the tenant regularly called the police to complain about the noise, and on a few occasions managed to get a social event shut down on the weekdays, causing the club a significant headache. In return, empty bottles and the odd broken bottle turned up on the tenant's porch, making the tenant feel like he was being targeted. The tenant applied for an injunction to prevent all members of the club from coming near his apartment, but without proof of who had broken the bottles was not successful. The tenant then wrote a letter to the liquor control board requesting that the club's license to serve alcohol be suspended because of the negative impact the club was having on the neighbourhood. His complaint was accepted and assigned to an investigator. The club served notice on the tenant that they were filing a lawsuit to stop his harassment of the club.

The I/R/P Model Diagnosis and Worksheet: The Greek Social Club

1. Assess the type of processes used so far by the parties and the outcomes that they've been getting.

Interest-Based Processes Used:	Outcomes:
• The initial attempt by the tenant to talk to the club was to try to get his interests met	• It failed. The club fell back on their "rights," i.e., the bylaw, and didn't consider the tenant's interests at all.
Rights-Based Processes Used:	**Outcomes:**
• The club relied solely on the bylaw, rather than pay any attention to the tenant's concerns. • The tenant applied for injunctions but didn't succeed. • The tenant tried to have the liquor license revoked, and that is in process. • The club is considering a lawsuit over the "harassment."	• These processes served only to escalate the situation, polarizing the parties further. Each party has spent a great deal of time and effort (as well as money) trying to assert their rights over the rights of the other party, so far to no avail.

(Continued)

Power-Based Processes Used:	Outcomes:
• The tenant has repeatedly called police, trying to invoke an authority with some power to solve the problem. • Some club members have tried to intimidate the tenant by leaving bottles or broken bottles on his porch, to try and get him to back down.	• The power-based processes have again only escalated the situation, leaving both parties feeling threatened and vulnerable. This makes resolution more and more difficult.

The I/R/P Model Strategic Direction: The Greek Social Club

2. Develop options for Interest-based processes that may help the parties:

Interest-based options require looking at what both parties want and need, and focusing on the constructive interests the parties have.[6] By looking at what each party really wants (as opposed to the newly created interests of revenge and punishing each other) the parties can better look for solutions that will actually solve the problem.

The most obvious processes to do this would be finding a way for the two parties to sit down and negotiate, to listen to and understand what each of them really need out of this. Either party could initiate this. Should that not work, a second option would be some form of mediation. By asking a third party to organize and run the negotiation, it might make it easier for each party to feel safe in attending.[7]

6. Refer to Model #2 –Triangle of Satisfaction to help look at a full range of both parties' interests.
7. Refer to the Dynamics of Trust model for more. Using a neutral third party is a form of procedural trust that can be used when there is no interpersonal trust in the situation.

3. Identify low-cost Rights-based processes the parties should consider if Interest-based approaches fail:

Parties are headed for high-cost rights-based processes such as court or regulatory bodies like the liquor control board. If negotiation fails, a lower-cost rights-based option might be to get their local city councillor involved (or another person who both parties would respect), have him or her review the situation, and tell both parties what's reasonable. This might temper the anger that both parties are feeling, and help them re-think their point of view.

4. Identify low-cost Power-based processes the parties should consider if Rights-based processes should fail:

A lower cost option for the tenant than constantly calling police might be to start involving neighbours to bring community pressure to bear on the social club. The social club, on the other hand, could open its doors to the community more, put a function on that the entire street is invited to in an effort to build support. While both these approaches are risky (as all power-based processes are) in that it risks dividing the whole street and escalating the situation, it is probably better and lower cost than constant police calls and the "self-help" approach of broken bottles on the tenant's porch, which could easily lead to a violent confrontation between the tenant and other social club members.

5. Identify Opportunities to loop back:

This is a key step. Parties should look for ways to get back to the interest-based level by finding a way to meet and make the relationship actually work for both of them. They could do this by either party extending an olive branch and an offer to meet and talk. They could ask a third party, such as their city councillor or a local community figure, to sit down with them and facilitate a discussion. They could each appoint a representative (a lawyer, a friend, etc.) to negotiate on their behalf with instructions to find a way to meet both parties' important interests. Any of these strategies would shift the parties away from the aggressive, adversarial approach they have both been using (with little success), and focus them on actually solving the problem.

Epilogue of the Case Study

The police, fed up with being called about the matter, referred the case to a community mediation organization, which contacted both parties and asked if they would participate in mediation to try to resolve these issues. Reluctantly, both parties agreed.

After four hours of mediation (which included extensive venting by both parties and a clear identification of what each reasonably wanted to make this work), an agreement to minimize the problems was reached, along with a commitment to try it out for three months to see if it helped and to meet again if either party still had concerns. Over the course of a year and three additional meetings, the friction between the parties has stopped and all formal complaints have been withdrawn. In addition, the tenant has received a standing offer to drop by any of the club's social functions and join the party, an invitation the tenant has accepted a couple of times.

CHAPTER EIGHT

MODEL #5:
THE DYNAMICS OF TRUST

BACKGROUND OF THE TRUST MODEL

The Dynamics of Trust model was developed by the author incorporating the work of Daryl Landau.[1] A significant amount of research was conducted to develop this model in the area of Attribution Theory, a cornerstone in understanding the dynamics of trust in human interactions.

One of the core issues in conflict resolution between parties is the issue of trust. We often hear the phrase "I don't trust you," or "I don't trust them" when we manage conflict. Trust, or lack of it, can be a significant barrier to parties' finding a resolution to an issue; indeed, it can prevent the parties from even wanting to talk. On the other side of the coin, trust is a unique resource, in that trust is expanded rather than depleted the more it is used. The more we can access trust with the parties, the more useful and effective it becomes in reaching resolution. Trust is a key resource in the conflict management process.

Trust itself is one of the least understood "commodities" in human relationships. We often think of trust as a single thing,

1. Daryl Landau is a Toronto-based mediator and trainer in the field of conflict resolution.

a single measure, a single component, when this is patently not the case. For example, many of us get in a car and drive to work on roads and highways where the only thing separating us from oncoming cars is a white line painted on the road (and in many cases, not even a solid white line!). We are, in essence, trusting thousands of strangers to stay on their side of the line. If we didn't fundamentally trust that they would, it's virtually certain that no one would drive a car. Does this mean that we "trust" every stranger we pass on the road? We clearly trust them to stay on their side of the road, but we probably wouldn't trust them with the keys to our house. So we can trust someone in one situation, for one reason, and not necessarily trust them in all situations for all things. Trust, therefore, has a complex and varied dynamic in human relationships.

There are a variety of definitions of trust that approach the subject from different angles, from a psychological view to a personality view to a behavioural view. For our purposes, we'll look at a functional definition of trust to help us understand the dynamics surrounding it.

A simple definition of trust is having positive expectations about another's motives and intentions toward us where potential risk is involved.[2] The two key elements of this definition are these:

1. **Risk:** Risk is a key element of trust, in the sense that we have to take risks (small or large) to explore, test, and eventually build trust. Without actually relying on someone, without taking a small risk with them, we can never really know if we can trust them. A significant question, however, is given a choice, why would anyone ever take such a risk? The answer is simple: it's the only way to get what we want. If we needed nothing from each other, ever, there would be no need for trust in the first place. The reality, of course, is the opposite. The more interdependent we are, whether at work

---

2. A more complete definition would include not only motives and intentions, but also the other person's capability or competency. Since competency is a relatively objective measure (compared to measuring a person's motives), and since competency will be addressed in Attribution Theory, we'll work with motives and intentions here.

or in our personal lives, the more we rely on others, the more risk we must take. The level of trust we have in the situation or the people affects the size of the risk we'll take and how frequently we'll take those risks. Risk is integral to trust at all levels.

2. **Motives and Intentions:** The motives and intentions of other people are invisible to us, we can only infer or attribute motives based on their behaviour; or, more accurately, how we interpret their behaviour. When we assess another person's trustworthiness, we are assessing whether they have "good intentions," (that they care about the needs of others) or whether they have "bad intentions," (they are indifferent to others' needs, care only about themselves, or will actively harm other people for their own benefit). Our assignment of motives to other people is critical, because it also determines how we assign fault and blame. When conflict arises, how we decide who caused it, and therefore who is at fault and who is to blame, will determine what happens to our level of trust with the other party.

The Dynamics of Trust model, from a diagnostic point of view, focuses on these two areas:

1. The assessment of each party's level of risk tolerance relative to what they want or need, and
2. the assessment of causes and assignments of blame.

Risk and Risk Tolerance

Each person's level of risk tolerance is a complex balance of personality (our personal tendency to like risk, or not) and our past experience with (and perceptions of) similar situations. Not surprisingly, it has little to do with factual assessments of risk, because human beings are notoriously bad at assessing actual risk. For example, people going camping in the woods will tend to think about, perhaps even obsess about the risk of a bear attack, a risk that is statistically far lower than the chances of being struck by lightning. At the same time, they will get in their car and drive 300 miles to reach the campground without thinking about or considering the fact that driving is by far one of the most dangerous activities we ever do.

Risk tolerance, however, is not based solely on personality or perception; it is also based on the relationship between the fear of what might be lost (the risk) compared to the benefit of what might be gained (the reward). It is the party's assessment of this risk/reward balance that determines behaviour.

In simple terms, if the risk or loss is seen as greater than the reward or gain, the party is not likely to take the risk unless they have sufficiently positive expectations about the other party's motives and intentions; in other words, unless there is sufficient trust. This leads us to look in depth at the second component of trust—how we assess motives and assign blame.

Causes and Blame: Attribution Theory and Self-Serving Bias

Attribution Theory is a cornerstone in the broader discipline of psychology, and has been the subject of significant amounts of research and writing over the last 30 years.

Essentially, what Attribution Theory says is this: When a negative event arises, when we are hurt or harmed, we begin by attributing the cause to someone or something. We do this in order to make sense of what has happened. And we have a strong tendency to attribute in a particular way.

Attribution to Self

When we are involved with or cause a negative event, we have a strong tendency to attribute the cause to the *situation*, such as lack of information, lack of training (that should have been given to us), orders from our boss that we had no choice about, market forces, or other circumstances that we see as beyond our control. In essence, we attribute the best of intentions to ourselves and blame outside circumstances for the problem, thus minimizing the fault or blame.

Attribution to Others

When *others* are involved with or cause a negative event, we have a strong tendency to ignore (or minimize) the situational factors and attribute the cause to the intrinsic nature or bad intentions of the other person. In other words, we lay fault and blame on the other individual personally; we attribute the cause to their innate bad character, their indifference, even their obvious bad intentions. We give ourselves the benefit of the doubt (big time), but do not give that to others.

Psychologists have demonstrated this tendency so strongly that they refer to this as "self-serving or egocentric bias." The research has found this bias to be strong and pronounced in virtually all studies done on how we attribute fault and blame.

Effect of Self-Serving Bias on Trust

This self-serving bias has a profound effect on trust. It means that in many situations, the negative events are attributed in a way that exaggerates the wrong, invents bad intentions, blames the other party to the point of feeling betrayed, and makes the conflict deeply personal. All of this happens because of the assumptions driven by the self-serving bias and not because of what is necessarily true.

The effect on trust is dramatic. Negative attributions and blame magnify the "risk" side of the equation and minimize the possibility of any reward, making any amount of trust almost impossible. Clearly, a practitioner must understand the dynamics of attribution and blame to work effectively with trust in conflict situations.

DIAGNOSIS WITH THE TRUST MODEL

What Attribution Theory highlights is that there is a whole range of attributions that people are capable of making in a given situation (albeit with a bias toward blaming others rather than oneself). From a practitioner point of view, the Dynamics of Trust model will help us diagnose the underlying attributions that are perpetuating the conflict. Diagnostically, then, the Trust Model says that there are fundamentally three types of attributions people can make in conflict situations:

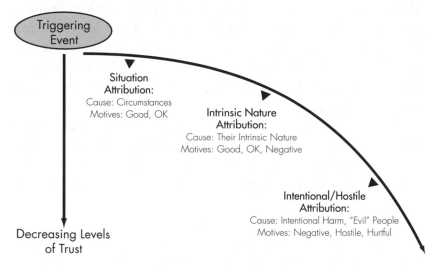

Situation Attribution

When we attribute the cause of the conflict or problem to the situation or circumstances (which we often do when attributing causes to ourselves), we are saying that the cause was due to factors beyond the person's control or skill level. The intentions were good, they tried their best, and the outcome was not desired by anyone. Some of the beliefs that this type of attribution tends to generate are:

• Circumstances outside of the person's control caused the problem, or forced the person into doing what they did;

- Their lack of skill or knowledge, or lack of accurate information, caused the problem;
- It's not their fault, these circumstances were largely beyond their control;
- The person did their best in spite of lacking information, knowledge, or skill needed;
- The problem they caused is not indicative of their nature or character;
- The person is blamed very little, if at all;
- The intentions attributed range from good to okay;
- This is probably a good person, who may need help;
- The person's actions were not aimed personally at us in any way.

Some examples of a Situation attribution are:

- A boss fires three employees because the company is close to bankruptcy and he doesn't have any other option.
- A person kills an intruder or attacker purely in self-defence.
- A person rear-ends the car in front because of black ice on the road.
- A clerk makes a mistake because he was never trained properly on the computer system.

This attribution results in relatively low levels of blame, maintains higher levels of trust, and gives parties a strong sense that this problem can be prevented in the future if it's properly addressed.

Intrinsic Nature Attribution

This attribution covers a wide range, but essentially attributes the conflict to the intrinsic nature of the other person. It may be because they're shy, it may be because of their culture or traditions, it may be that past experiences or core values have strongly affected them, it may be that they simply don't pay attention to other people, but in all cases the cause is attributed to the other person's innate character or nature rather than to conscious, intentional behaviour. Some beliefs that this type of attribution tends to generate are:

- The person caused the harm because of their intrinsic qualities: personality, culture, values, past experience;
- The person's intrinsic nature can be seen as benign, or can be seen as dangerous;
- It may or may not be their fault, the harm or conflict was not necessarily intentional, it was more a byproduct of their intrinsic qualities;
- The person may or may not be aware of the harm or the impact on the other person;
- Blame can range from very low to medium-high;
- Intentions attributed can range from good all the way to negative.

Some examples of an Intrinsic Nature attribution are:

- A manager who steps on people's toes because she is a workaholic committed to meeting the team's goals and objectives;
- A child or a mentally incompetent person who starts a fire that injures someone;
- An employee who doesn't address a problem because he simply cannot deal with confrontation of any kind;
- Parents who push their children incessantly to go to university because they never had the chance themselves;
- A friend who betrays a trust because he or she is incapable of keeping a secret.

When parties make an Intrinsic Nature attribution it's usually more personal than a Situation attribution, but is typically less personal than an Intentional attribution. Where our attribution lands in this range is based on our assessment of how dangerous these intrinsic qualities are.[3] In many cases, an Intrinsic Nature attribution allows significant levels of trust to remain, frequently in parts of the relationship unrelated to the conflict.

Intentional/Hostile Attribution

This is the most destructive form of attribution in that it lays complete blame on the other person. It sees their actions as intentionally causing harm, either because they are hostile toward us or they gain in some way by harming us. It assumes that the other person knew what damage their actions would cause, and proceeded anyway. It assumes intentional dishonesty, meanness, and hostility. Some beliefs that this type of attribution tends to generate are:

- The person intentionally caused the harm, for personal gain or advantage;
- The circumstances and choices causing the conflict or harm are fully in the person's control and choice;
- Full blame is attributed to the person;
- Intentions attributed range from negative to evil;
- The person is a "bad person," i.e., morally deficient, unethical, etc.
- The actions were aimed personally and directly at us.

Some examples of Intentional attribution are:

- An insurance claimant who is lying to collect on the insurance policy;
- Bosses who degrade employees in front of the team because they enjoy using their power, or to simply "teach them who is boss";

3. In some cases, if the intrinsic quality is extreme, such as deep racism, there will be no trust at all, in spite of an intrinsic attribution tending to be less trust-breaking than an intentional attribution.

- A boss who fires an employee to make himself look good and get promoted;
- A person who deliberately breaks a contract because he or she found a cheaper price elsewhere;
- A friend who betrays a trust for personal gain.

This attribution results in very high levels of blame, eliminates trust, and brings a strong sense that any further dealings with this party are too risky and dangerous, including any attempts at resolution.

Attribution and Blame

There is a strong correlation between the type of attribution we make and the laying of blame. In general, the Situation attribution minimizes the laying of blame on the other party and depersonalizes the situation; the Intrinsic attribution causes a low-to-moderate level of blame along with a moderate amount of "taking it personally," and the Intentional attribution lays a significant amount of blame that feels highly personal. It can be arranged on the scale as follows:

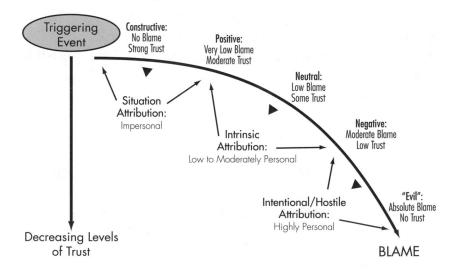

How Attributions Form

Motives and intentions cannot be seen, they can only be inferred from our interpretation of the other party's behaviour. Attributions, therefore, are fundamentally perceptions, not reality. Perceptions are influenced mostly by two factors: information and preconceptions.

- Information, or data, can greatly influence the attributions made.[4] Mis-information, lack of information, different interpretations of information, and even too much information make it difficult to evaluate the situation. Nevertheless, we must evaluate the situation in order to make sense of it. This evaluation is done, therefore, by selecting the information that supports one view of the situation and rejecting or ignoring the information that contradicts that view.

- Preconceptions refer to the values, beliefs, past experiences, stereotypes, and assumptions that we all carry. While most of us accept the phrase "Seeing is believing," numerous studies have shown that the reverse is more commonly true, that in fact "Believing is seeing." This means that whatever we already believe is what we tend to see. If we believe our friend is lazy, for example, we attribute her being 15 minutes late to that belief, ignoring the obvious fact that it's rush hour or that it's snowing outside.

Still, attributions can be changed. As practitioners, we can help to influence parties' attributions by working with or challenging the two elements that form these attributions, namely, information and preconceptions. We'll explore that process in the Strategic section of this model.

Summary of Attributions

The Trust model clearly shows us the following:

---

4. For an in-depth look at how data contributes to conflict, refer to the Circle of Conflict model and the Data slice.

- The attributions each party (including ourselves) makes in a given situation dramatically influence the behaviour of each party toward the other;
- Some attributions maintain trust between the parties, and some not only destroy trust, they also prevent any rebuilding of trust;
- Attributions are frequently based on incomplete or incorrect information, along with preconceptions and stereotypes;
- Attributions can be changed.

How we work with the parties' attributions will greatly influence the outcome of the conflict.

CASE STUDY: TRUST MODEL DIAGNOSIS

In our Case Study we can apply the Trust model to diagnose the parties' attributions, and by doing this begin to understand the source and level of mistrust and blame each party is dealing with in the situation.

Applying the Dynamics of Trust to our Case Study, the attributions might look this way:

Bob's Attributions to:

Sally

- Bob attributes the loss in the competition to a bias against him from Sally, believing that the competition was set up so that Diane would win and he would lose. (Intentional attribution to Sally.)
- Bob also believes that Sally is creating the AS-1 role just to favour Diane, because both of them are female and "women always stick together." (Intrinsic and Intentional attribution.)
- Bob also believes that Sally dislikes him and wants to have no communication or contact with him, which is why all contact is being routed through Diane. (Intentional attribution.)

In looking at these high levels of Intentional and strong Intrinsic attributions, Bob believes Sally has personally caused this conflict and has assigned a high degree of blame to Sally for the current situation.

Diane

- Bob doesn't seem to have too much of an issue with Diane personally, because he attributes the problems to Sally, not to Diane. Diane, he believes, is just trying to do her job as ordered. (Situation attribution.)
- Bob believes that Diane is supporting Sally in part because "women always stick together," but in Diane's case, he views this as Intrinsic only, and not Intentional.
- Diane gets frustrated with Bob at times, which Bob attributes to a lack of ability on Diane's part when it comes to accounting issues, something he's expert at and she isn't, since she tends to focus on client service issues. (Situation attribution.)

Since most attributions toward Diane are Situation or mildly Intrinsic, Bob has little or no blame to lay on Diane for the conflict. He attributes little of the cause to Diane personally, even though the daily interactions with Diane are tense and negative.

Sally's Attributions to:

Bob

- Sally is frustrated that Bob won't listen to what she has ordered him to do. She attributes this to Bob having an "entitlement" mentality, and being incapable of seeing that he's not the best candidate for the job. (Intrinsic attribution.)
- Sally believes that Bob just doesn't have the people skills to be an AS-1. (Intrinsic attribution.)

- Sally also believes Bob has not recognized where he lacks skills because he is too proud to admit any faults. (Intrinsic attribution).
- Sally believes that Bob is trying to upset her and frustrate her enough that she'll eventually promote him, or re-run the competition. (Intentional attribution.)
- Sally also believes Bob doesn't like losing, and that this is understandable since no one likes losing. (Intrinsic attribution.)
- Finally, Sally believes that others in the department are encouraging Bob to rebel to try to derail all of her changes, and these other people are manipulating Bob. (Situation attribution.)

Sally clearly believes Bob has caused the current situation. That said, since most of the attributions are Intrinsic or Situation, Sally is only moderate in taking the situation personally and in blaming Bob on a personal level.

Diane

- Sally believes that Diane is a good person, and is behaving poorly out of frustration with the difficult situation she has been put in. (Situation attribution.)

Sally has little, if any, blame for Diane since the attribution is purely Situational.

Diane's Attributions to:

Bob

- Diane believes that Bob is angry at Sally more than her, but that she is paying the price because of her promotion. Bob would have been angry with anyone in her position. (Situation attribution.)

- Diane thinks Bob is somewhat sexist and doesn't like women for bosses, and suddenly he has two of them, which is part of the problem. She also believes he is "from the older generation, and can't help it." (Intrinsic attribution.)
- Diane also believes that Bob is frustrated with some of the tasks she has assigned him to learn, since he is not comfortable in a customer service role. (Situation attribution.)

While Diane is very frustrated and believes Bob is behaving poorly, she assesses only a low or moderate amount of blame to Bob, based on the mainly Situation and low Intrinsic attributions she is making.

Sally

- Diane thinks that Sally has been thrown in the lion's den unfairly by *her* boss and that Sally isn't getting much support for the changes she's trying to implement. (Situation attribution.)
- Diane thinks that Sally has moved too fast and pushed people too hard, both because Sally is impatient and likes to get things done and because she doesn't have a choice in this, since her boss expects it (Intrinsic and Situation attribution).

Although she recognizes that Sally's actions are contributing to the current problems, Diane has assigned very little blame to Sally, due to the mainly Situation and relatively positive Intrinsic attributions made.

Based on the analysis above, it becomes clear that while everyone is frustrated, Bob has taken the situation deeply personally, Diane only a little bit personally, and Sally sees the problem both as a situational problem as well as a "Bob" problem. Bob has attributed the cause of the situation primarily to Intentional reasons on Sally's part, with a negative Intrinsic attribution supporting that. Sally, on the other hand, has attributed the cause mostly to neutral Intrinsic and Situation factors, i.e., Bob's nature and skill level, and only a little to Intentional causes. Diane, finally, thinks the whole problem is mostly Situation, with some Intrinsic issues with Bob.

Note how the attributions for each party are dramatically different. In the next section we'll see how effective practice based on this model can address these differing attributions.

STRATEGIC DIRECTION FROM THE TRUST MODEL

Now that we understand roughly what each of the parties believes to be the cause of the conflict, the Trust model can offer the practitioner a range of strategies for how he or she may proceed. Before moving on to strategies, however, we need to look at two different types of trust and some of their characteristics.

The Trust model identifies two broad types of trust that parties are always relying on: interpersonal trust and procedural trust.

Interpersonal Trust

Interpersonal trust is a set of feelings that defines how comfortable we are taking a given level of risk with a specific person. This has to do with our judgement of that person's character, integrity, values, and so on. It answers the question, "How much do I trust this individual?" Some characteristics of interpersonal trust are:

- This is the strongest form of trust;
- Usually based on belief and assumption and less on actual information (we just know that they can be trusted);

- Inconsistent behaviour may have absolutely no effect on trust (I know they must have had a very good reason for doing that);
- With interpersonal trust, parties tend to assume the motives of the other person are good;
- Parties are anticipating success in the relationship as a way to validate their decision to trust;
- Based on perceived common values and common interests, to a large degree;
- Examples of strong interpersonal trust include doing business on a handshake, sharing information with a close friend that could harm us if revealed, sharing sensitive information in a negotiation because we have worked with the other party before, loaning money to a colleague, etc.

People tend to assume that interpersonal trust is what "trust" means, in that if I don't trust you on an interpersonal basis, then there is no "trust." In reality, this is only one (albeit important) form of trust. It should also be clear that interpersonal trust is difficult to achieve and easy to lose. It is impossible for people to "will" interpersonal trust, meaning that interpersonal trust is built on experience and is not achieved by simply agreeing to "trust" each other.

Procedural Trust

Procedural trust is the trust we place in a structure or process we are involved in, as opposed to the individual. For example, parties often attempt mediation when they have very little trust in each other, and may have little experience with the mediator as well. In this case, they are placing their trust in the mediation process itself. It answers the question, "How much trust do I have in the process itself, regardless of the individual(s) involved?" Some characteristics of procedural trust are:

- This is limited, situation-specific trust and tends to be more fragile than interpersonal trust;
- Procedural trust is broken by unexpected or inconsistent behaviour;
- Based on trust in the structures surrounding the individuals involved (Are they licensed or trained? Do they have credentials? Have the drugs been tested and approved by the government?);
- Based on monitoring (a third party monitors and verifies the quality of the work; the manager monitors the employees' arrival time to verify attendance);
- Based on deterrence (I don't pay you until the work is completed);
- Parties tend to assume the motives of the other person are either selfish or uncaring of others, which is why the procedural trust is needed in the first place;
- Parties are anticipating failure as a way to protect themselves;
- Examples of procedural trust include the process of buying a house, where the purchase money and the deed are exchanged through a trusted third party (such as a lawyer or a title company); court-supervised visits with children where the marital relationship has broken down; having a facilitator or mediator manage the negotiation to ensure that neither side does anything unfair or unreasonable.

Procedural trust is significantly different from interpersonal trust, in that procedural trust processes can be collaboratively built and agreed by the parties themselves. Procedural trust is not a matter of will; it is a set of steps or structures that are tangible and defined. This makes procedural trust a powerful tool when working with conflict, and when applying some of the strategies below.

Strategy #1 – Focus on Procedural Trust, not Interpersonal Trust

One of the first casualties in conflict is the loss of trust, but how much trust is lost and how the practitioner should proceed is best assessed by looking at the attributions that the parties are making. In extreme conflict, both interpersonal trust as well as procedural trust can be lost. In these cases, parties simply don't want to deal with the other party because they can't see a safe way to negotiate with an untrustworthy party. For this reason, Strategy #1 is to focus the parties away from interpersonal trust (which can be seen as so risky to the parties as to be inconceivable) and focus them on various forms of procedural trust, on a process that will effectively protect both parties' interests enough to begin discussions and move forward.

How exactly to move forward can be decided by looking at the attributions that are in play for the parties. The attributions the parties have made will direct the practitioner toward the different steps that may be effective.

Procedural Trust and Confidence Building Measures (CBMs)

Interpersonal and procedural trust are directly linked to the attributions the parties have made. In general, Situation attributions maintain the most interpersonal trust and require the least procedural trust; Intrinsic attributions damage interpersonal trust and require some level of procedural trust, while Intentional attributions destroy interpersonal trust and require an almost exclusive focus on procedural trust to move forward.

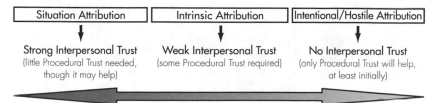

Situation Attribution	Intrinsic Attribution	Intentional/Hostile Attribution
↓	↓	↓
Strong Interpersonal Trust	Weak Interpersonal Trust	No Interpersonal Trust
(little Procedural Trust needed, though it may help)	(some Procedural Trust required)	(only Procedural Trust will help, at least initially)

Since conflict is extremely destructive to interpersonal trust, the more blame and negative attribution the parties make toward each other, the more we need to look toward procedural trust to help the parties move forward. In other words, by implementing procedural trust effectively we can help the parties rebuild some interpersonal trust down the road.

The first step in implementing procedural trust is to create a safe environment to begin the negotiation. This means shifting completely away from any substantive negotiation and focusing on the negotiation process itself.[5] Procedural trust often focuses on who will attend, what will be on the agenda, what will be confidential, how the process will be monitored and made safe for everyone, how agreements (if reached) will be monitored, what the future relationships might look like, and so on. Gaining agreement to important procedural elements often lays the groundwork for effective substantive negotiations. Another strategy to build enough procedural trust to move parties forward is by encouraging the use of "confidence building measures (CBMs)."

Confidence Building Measures

Procedural Trust:	Confidence Building Measures:	Increase in Interpersonal Trust:
• Monitoring • Third Party Help • Mutual Deterrence • Risk/Reward Analysis • Steps taken with independent verification that requires little interpersonal trust to commit to, i.e., no/low risk.	• Unilateral steps taken by one party to show good faith and to test the good faith of the other party • Once parties see each other performing as they said they would, it encourages parties to take greater risks with each other in the future.	• Parties see each other taking risks, fulfilling commitments • Parties build history of trustworthiness between themselves over time.

5. In the language of the Triangle of Satisfaction, this is a shift away from Result interests to focus on Process and Psychological interests.

Confidence building measures are small steps taken by one or both parties that signal a readiness to unilaterally demonstrate trust to the other side. They are actions taken beyond what is needed to establish basic procedural trust. A confidence building measure is an action that does not ask the other side to place their confidence in us, but shows that we are prepared to place some confidence (or trust) in them. By taking a small risk and "going first," it creates a positive pressure on the other party to reciprocate. CBM's often break negotiating logjams and create a pattern of important procedural trust steps.

Examples of confidence building measures can include:

- In a construction dispute, one side offering to resume work on site today, provided the other side makes a partial payment within a week.
- In a supplier dispute, the manufacturer waiving the requirement for cash up front by offering to ship small orders on a 15-day payment basis.
- In a workplace dispute, the manager offering the employee his or her previous position back provided the employee attends certain training courses within two months.

In each of the examples above, one side was prepared to take a risk and go first; in doing so, they created a situation where if the other side didn't reciprocate, it would be clear who the difficult party was. This dynamic creates a positive pressure on both parties to behave well. When parties begin to see each other as reliable through effective use of procedural trust and confidence building measures, they will begin to rebuild interpersonal trust, slowly reducing the need for CBMs or the need for extensive procedural trust structures in the future.

Strategy #2: Attributional Retraining

The second strategy to deal with negative attributions is to directly address the attribution made by each party about the other. This strategy applies where there is an abundance of Intrinsic or Intentional attributions.

As previously noted, whenever attributions are made, they are based on assumptions, on interpreting the information in a particular way. Parties frequently take the same information yet arrive at very different attributions and conclusions.

A good analogy is a children's connect-the-dots game, where a series of numbered dots are printed on a page but form no obvious picture. By connecting the dots in the right order (which is helped by the fact that the dots are numbered), a picture such as a dog or house emerges. In real life, when we assess conflict situations we are presented with the same series of "dots" (in this case, data points such as experiences, feelings, events, etc.) only in our case without the numbering. In Figure 1 below, to draw a "picture" we have to find a way to connect the dots that makes sense to us.

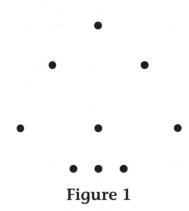

Figure 1

In Figure 2, however, the same data points (dots) are connected in different ways, leading to very different pictures.

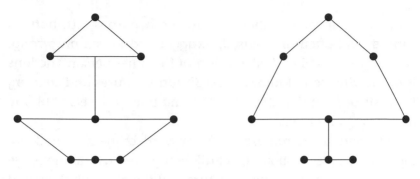

Figure 2

To complicate matters even further, now imagine the situation where some dots (or data points) exist in one person's picture while others only exist in the other person's picture (each party having information the other doesn't have, or attributing different reasons for the events or information). Finally, as in Figure 3, it is not uncommon for a party to draw a picture that simply ignores some of the data points, since they don't fit the picture the party has created or assumed. Completely different pictures can then be created, each of which will be completely legitimate (even see as exclusively "right") to the party drawing it. Our assumptions, our attribution of motives, our interpretation of the situation and the other party's behaviour become highly influential in how we see and feel about the other party.

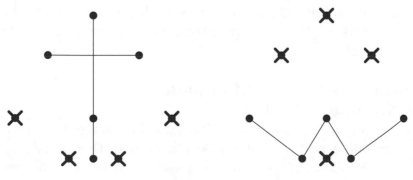

Figure 3

What this all means, then, is that both parties' attributions can be, and often are, biased, exaggerated, or simply wrong. Frequently, this biased attribution of the other person's actions is in the direction of minimizing Situation causes and creating Intrinsic or Intentional causes, leading to high levels of blame and strong emotions.

Attributional retraining is a fancy word for (gently) challenging a party's assumptions. By challenging these assumptions, we help the party change their "picture"—if the dots that they used to draw the picture of the boat no longer exist, they will need to find a new picture to make sense of the situation. This process can help them shift from Intentional attribution and strong blame, to Intrinsic attribution and less blame, or even to seeing some Situation attribution and eliminating some blame altogether. This can significantly de-escalate the conflict and introduce enough trust to move forward (even if it is procedural trust at first).

CASE STUDY: TRUST MODEL STRATEGIC DIRECTION

Having diagnosed the situation for what kind of attributions have been made, it becomes clear that the strongest and most negative attributions are between Bob and Sally, and it is the strength of these negative attributions that is preventing any kind of solution. This means that a first step might be to work on the negative attributions that Bob has made about Sally.

Strategy # 2: Use Attributional Retraining with Bob

The mediator meets with Bob alone, and begins unpacking the assumptions and attributions Bob has made. This is done by asking Bob some of the following questions, all of which uncover and challenge (gently) the assumptions Bob has made:

- You feel that Sally biased the competition to Diane. Given that she didn't sit on the competition panel, how did she do this? (Bob: *She spoke with the panel, that's how.*) When did she do this? (*I don't know. She just must have.*) Why doesn't the union feel this competition was biased? (*They're on her side*). If they were on her side, why did they make her re-run the competition? Why didn't they just let the first one stand? (*Well, I don't know*).

- You feel that Sally doesn't want to have anything to do with you, and that's why she wants everything to go through Diane, is that it? (*Yes, it's just a way of ignoring me because she doesn't like me.*) Why do you want contact with her? (*I want to know what's going on, because I'm important around here too.*) How would your view change if Sally, knowing this was important to you, were to keep your direct communication lines open? (*She won't!*) And if she did, what would that tell you? (*Well, I don't know, that maybe she's rethought some of this?*)

- You believe that Sally is inventing the AS-1 role as a way of rewarding or helping Diane, because she is female, too. (*Yes, they all stick together.*) How clear are you that the director, Sally's boss, has ordered this position created in offices across the country, that Sally had nothing to do with this decision? (*What? Where did you hear that?*) From Sally. How could you verify that? (*I can call other offices to find out, I guess*) And if that is true, how would that change your view of why Sally is making these changes? (*Well, I'd have to think about it.*)

The above dialogue is an example of attributional retraining, introducing information and interpretations other than the ones Bob has made, and effectively causing Bob to rethink some of his attributions. If Sally had nothing to do with creating the position, Bob will have to rethink his view of Sally in some way, and that's the goal of attributional retraining. This can take a bit of time, but can substantially alter the way each party views the underlying reasons for the other party behaving the way they are.

Strategy #2: Use Attributional Retraining with Sally

The mediator meets with Sally alone, and begins unpacking the assumptions and attributions Sally has made. This is done by asking Sally some of the following questions, all of which uncover and challenge (gently) the assumptions she has made:

- You feel that Bob is behaving this way because he wants to frustrate you to the point you'll either promote him, or redo the competition again, is that it? (Sally: *Yes, he's doing this just to make my life difficult!*) In general, how good a job had Bob been doing before all of this? (*Well, he did a good job here for a long time before I arrived.*) What if the reason he's behaving badly is because he really cares about his job, and needs some contact with you to feel that he's in the loop, and doing a good job? How would you feel about helping him? (*I'm willing to help, but he has to stop being such a problem.*) If he were willing to behave well, what contact would you offer so he felt important and included? (*I'd certainly consider any suggestions, if that's really the problem!*)
- You think that Bob hasn't recognized he lacks a number of skills. (*That's right. He's too proud to see that.*) When has Bob ever refused to go on training that was offered to him? (*Well, he hasn't refused with me, but I haven't offered anything.*) How would it change your thinking if you offered him some skills training, and he accepted it? (*It would show me he was interested in improving his work. . . .*)

In both cases, this would start the process of changing the underlying attributions and assumptions that were blocking and preventing any trust building between the parties.

Next, let's look at how procedural trust and confidence building measures might help.

Strategy #1: Focus on Procedural Trust

After shifting some of the hard-line attributions between Sally and Bob, the parties looked at what steps could be taken to start improving things. They focused on two areas, communication and skills improvement.

Communication

After the attributional retraining step, Sally started to accept that Bob wanted communication with her to continue to feel that he was important and was doing a good job. Bob started to accept that Sally wanted communications to go through Diane to help free up her time for management-type work. Bob then suggested that Sally copy him with all communications that went to Diane; this would keep him in the loop with no additional time to Sally. Sally agreed (a confidence building measure), and asked that any communication back from Bob go first through Diane, and only if there was something that Diane couldn't help with that Bob contact Sally. Bob agreed (another confidence building measure), but asked that once in a while he be able to speak with Sally about the workplace in general, and that he feel comfortable in doing this. Sally agreed, as long as "once in a while" meant about once per month. Bob agreed.

Both Sally and Bob agreed to run it this way for two months, keep track of how many times Bob and Sally interacted, and assess how Bob felt working with Diane. At that point, Bob and Sally would meet to discuss how it was working and what needed changing. By structuring it as a "pilot" process, one that was open to change later, this was seen as lower risk for Bob in that he wasn't accepting this solution regardless of how it worked for him. Sally saw it as a way of making sure the changes didn't eat up too much of her time. For both, this pilot phase was seen as a way to build confidence in their decisions.

In essence, by making the changes a "pilot" process, Sally and Bob were jointly engaged in "verifying" that this approach would work. This was a process both of them could place trust in, indicating that this step was an effective use of procedural trust.

Skills Improvement

After the attributional retraining, Sally started to see Bob as having some ambition to improve his skills, and maybe interested in applying for other promotions. Bob started to see Sally as perhaps wanting him to do well in his job, and willing to help and support him in that.

Bob identified what skills he'd like to focus on, and Sally added one or two to that list. Sally committed to finding some training in the company that Bob could take, along with the budget for it. Both agreed to sit down with Diane after the training to create an assessment process to see if the training had helped; both agreed to log improvements to Bob's skills and performance. This made Bob feel that he was supported and helped in the workplace instead of targeted for attack; Sally felt this would show her that Bob did care about doing a good job. They even began to talk about what help Bob could ask for if he wanted to apply for other promotions.

In this case, the process of jointly building the skills improvement list and sending Bob on training were seen as confidence-building measures by both Sally and Bob. The assessment process was seen as the trust-monitoring process for Sally, while the training budget was seen as the trust-monitoring process for Bob. In both cases, this allowed each of them to verify that the other person was doing what they said they would do.

As you can see from the above, the practitioner focused first on some attributional retraining, and once that had some impact moved the parties to steps that relied on procedural trust and confidence building measures. These, in turn, began to create a small amount of interpersonal trust (or the possibility of it down the road), all of which contributed to moving the parties toward constructive resolution of the issues.

ASSESSING AND APPLYING THE TRUST MODEL

The Dynamics of Trust model is one of the most important models in conflict resolution work, since trust is foundational to human relationships.

Diagnostically, the Trust model goes to the heart of understanding where breaches of trust come from and what magnifies or exaggerates them in conflict settings. Attribution theory has long been researched and used to explain human behaviour. The Trust model applies it specifically to conflict settings by illuminating how the dynamic of self-serving bias plays a major role in sustaining and fuelling conflict. Finally, since the model gives practitioners a framework for understanding how parties perceive the conflict and make sense of the situation, it gives practitioners a powerful tool for diagnosing complex situations. The model rates very high on the diagnostic scale.

Strategically, the model also gives clear and strong direction for working with damaging attributions. By identifying attributional retraining (another form of reality testing) and focusing on procedural trust in conjunction with confidence building measures, it gives practitioners clear direction on how best to work with trust issues in conflict. It therefore rates high on the strategic scale.

PRACTITIONER'S WORKSHEET FOR THE TRUST MODEL

1. Diagnosis: Identify the type of attributions each party is making in the situation:

Party A	Party B
Situation Attributions: What is Party A attributing to circumstances beyond the control of Party B?	**Situation Attributions:** What is Party B attributing to circumstances beyond the control of Party A?
Intrinsic Nature Attributions: What is Party A attributing to Party B's nature or disposition?	**Intrinsic Nature Attributions:** What is Party B attributing to Party A's nature or disposition?
Intentional or Hostile Attributions: What does Party A believe Party B has done to cause intentional harm?	**Intentional or Hostile Attributions:** What does Party B believe Party A has done to cause intentional harm?

1a. What Situation or Intrinsic attributions are being missed by either party?

1b. What "Attributional Retraining" can be done to bring forward this information?

2. What Procedural Trust and Confidence Building Measures would help each party start to rebuild trust?

What CBMs from Party B would have impact with Party A?
What CBMs from Party A would have impact with Party B?
Who could be an effective "monitor" between Party A and Party B in the short term?
What would need to be monitored or verified so both parties felt that the process was safe and fair?

ADDITIONAL CASE STUDY: TRUST MODEL

Case Study: Co-Worker's Dilemma

This situation involved two co-workers, Jean and Anna. Jean had been in the department for about five years; Anna had been there about 15 years. Initially, when Jean joined the department, they got along reasonably well. About three years ago, Jean was given an "Acting Supervisor" appointment in the department and had to supervise Anna, along with two other employees, for about three months. Anna resented Jean's style of supervising, and the working relationship began to deteriorate.

The triggering event was this: Jean approached the manager, Sheri, saying that Anna's work quality was very poor, and Jean's work was suffering as a result. Jean relied on Anna (as well as two other staff) to supply reports and data to her. Sheri asked her to gather some information on "what was going on in the area" so she could address any problems. Jean took this to mean that she was to track Anna's work quality, and to do this she built an Excel spreadsheet detailing the dates requests were made to Anna, when the data was delivered, when scheduled reports were completed, and the quality of the work overall. In addition, she had included a "Comments" section that had the occasional comment such as "Late again!!" or "Quality?!" as a reflection of her frustration with Anna's work. It also included the odd comment about good quality work that Anna had done. She kept this spreadsheet for about two months on a network drive that some people on the team, but not Anna, had access to.

At about the two-month mark, and before Jean could share this information with Sheri, Anna found the file accidentally as she had always had access to this particular network drive (unbeknownst to Jean). She stormed into Sheri's office with the file and demanded to know what was going on. Sheri told her that the file Jean had created was unacceptable and she would address it with Jean. Anna stormed out, angrily yelled something at Jean, and threatened to file a harassment complaint against Jean unless Jean was disciplined. Jean, in Anna's mind, had been out to "to get her" for a while now, and this was evidence of Jean trying to get her fired.

Jean was upset as well. Jean, for her part, felt that she had just done what Sheri had asked her to do and was not trying to "get" Anna; she just wanted the quality of the work from Anna to improve so she could do her job properly. Jean took great pride in doing more than was expected of her. Workloads were increasing and she was falling behind due to Anna. When she approached Anna for information on reports, Anna ignored her or got angry. Jean didn't really accept that the comments on her spreadsheet were inappropriate, but she did realize that leaving the document on the network drive was a poor choice, since it wasn't secure.

Relations in the workplace plummeted. Anna went off on sick leave for a month, and upon her return didn't appear to feel any differently (Anna had been off on extended sick leave twice in the past year). Anna would not speak with Jean, and refused to sit down with Sheri and Jean in the same room. Co-workers began to complain about the workplace, about Anna's moods especially, and work fell way behind. Anna refused to have any contact with Jean, still convinced that Jean was out to get her. In addition, since Sheri had clearly not disciplined Jean, she began to feel that Sheri was taking Jean's side. She began talking to the union about filing a complaint or a grievance.

Trust Model Diagnosis and Worksheet: Co-Worker's Dilemma

Anna	Jean
Situation Attributions: *What is Anna attributing to circumstances beyond the control of Jean?* • Nothing. Anna attributes everything to Jean personally.	**Situation Attributions:** *What is Jean attributing to circumstances beyond the control of Anna?* • Nothing. Jean attributes most of this to Anna's lack of competence and her personality.
Intrinsic Nature Attributions: *What is Anna attributing to Jean's nature or disposition?* • Anna sees Jean as a workaholic with standards that are way too high.	**Intrinsic Nature Attributions:** *What is Jean attributing to Anna's nature or disposition?* • Jean thinks there is something mentally wrong with Anna beyond simple job stress. She thinks that Anna is a bit unbalanced.

Anna	Jean
Intentional or Hostile Attributions: *What does Anna believe Jean has done to intentionally harm her?*	**Intentional or Hostile Attributions:** *What does Jean believe Anna has done to intentionally harm her?*
• Anna believes that Jean is out to get her, to have her fired, and to humiliate her in the workplace. She believes Jean wrote that report and intended for others in the workplace to read it, to turn the rest of the department against her.	• Jean believes that for some reason, Anna is blaming her for all her problems, that she wants to make Jean the bad guy, and to publicly humiliate Jean.

Clearly, from the analysis, both parties have attributed the causes of the problem primarily to hostile and harmful intentions on each other's part, with a little bit of negative "intrinsic" attribution. This assessment was reflected in how emotionally "hot" the conflict was for both parties.

Trust Model Strategic Direction: Co-Worker's Dilemma
What Situation or Intrinsic attributions are being missed by either party?

Anna:
• Anna is not seeing the workload issues Jean is facing, and is not recognizing how much Jean relies on her work. (Situation)

- Anna hasn't clearly understood that Jean was asked to compile information on the work in the area and didn't undertake this on her own. (Situation)
- Anna is not recognizing that Jean has high standards and demands a lot of herself and that this, in general, is not a bad thing in the workplace. (Intrinsic)
- Anna is not recognizing that Jean's frustration is with not getting what she needs, and not directly with Anna personally. (Situation)
- Anna is not including the information that Jean had helped her quite a bit in the past. (Intrinsic)

Jean:
- Jean is not seeing that Anna may have a medical condition that may be affecting her emotionally (numerous sick leaves in the past year). (Intrinsic)
- Jean is not recognizing that Anna simply has a different work ethic than Jean does, but still has a work ethic that is in the range of acceptable in the workplace. (Intrinsic)
- Jean is not recognizing that it isn't her job or role to manage or judge Anna's work; it's her role to go to management if she's not getting what she needs to do her job well. (Situation)
- Jean is not recognizing that the comments are clearly inappropriate. (Situation)

What "Attributional Retraining" can be done to bring forward this information?

Questions for Anna:
- How clear are you that Sheri asked Jean to gather information about deadlines and workflows? That Jean, to a large degree, was doing what was asked of her?
- How much of the frustration you read in Jean's spreadsheet is because she felt frustrated in her own job, and not necessarily with you?

- If Jean is just out to get you, why would she have offered to, and indeed helped you, in the past?
- How much of this problem is because of the long hours and high standards Jean seems to impose on herself?

Questions for Jean:
- Anna has been off a few times in the past year; how much information do you have on that? (Assume none, since it's private information.) When people are off on leave a lot, is it usually due to vacation, or other reasons that may be somewhat stressful?
- When you feel frustrated that you're not getting reports or information you need, who is responsible for fixing that? (Answer: management.) What's the reason you're frustrated with Anna, when indeed it's management's responsibility to help you?
- How clear are you that Sheri believes the comments in your spreadsheet were inappropriate?
- You set high standards for quality of work, don't you? How appropriate or realistic is it to apply those standards to everyone in the workplace? Whose job is it to set standards for acceptable work for staff? How much of Anna's anger at you is because she feels you've been judging her work rather than letting management do it?

Procedural Trust Focus: What Confidence Building Measures would help each party start to rebuild?

What CBMs from Jean would have impact with Anna?
- Jean apologizing for the comments in the report.
- Jean providing verification that the report had been deleted and all copies destroyed. (In this case, only IT could delete files from the shared drive, and only at the request of the author of the file.)

- Jean's commitment to never gather information without Anna knowing (this CBM also needed to come from Sheri, as well as from Jean.)

What CBMs from Anna would have impact with Jean?

- For Jean, having Anna commit to behaving in civil, respectful ways whenever they had to interact in the workplace.
- Agreeing to not file a harassment complaint.

Who could be an effective "monitor" between Jean and Anna in the short term?

- It was agreed that there needed to be a buffer or monitor between Jean and Anna, at least for a while. Sheri was far too busy and acknowledged neglecting this department due to time pressure. Sheri decided to assign a supervisor to take over running the area, and it was agreed that the supervisor would be the buffer and monitor for the foreseeable future.

What would need to be monitored so both parties feel that the process is safe and fair?

- Parties agreed to meet with the supervisor and establish "ground rules" that the supervisor would then monitor and hold both Jean and Anna accountable for. The stated goal was to have this monitoring only a short-term process, after which Jean and Anna would manage their interactions themselves.

Epilogue of the Case Study

After initial meetings with Anna and Jean, the practitioner met with Sheri and arranged for Sheri to meet with Anna and Jean individually. This was to clearly articulate the following: To Anna, that it was Sheri who asked for the report, and not Jean choosing to do that on her own. Sheri apologized to Anna for not telling Anna, and took responsibility for that. To Jean, she made it clear that the comments in the spreadsheet were, in Sheri's view, inappropriate. After some discussion, Jean admitted she could see that they "didn't look good" to anyone else reading them.

The practitioner then met with Anna, who denied that she had been disrespectful in the past, but committed to behaving respectfully in the future. Anna agreed that it had to be respectful as defined by both Jean and the supervisor. Anna also agreed that if Jean apologized for the report, she would not file a harassment complaint. Through the "attributional retraining," she admitted that while she didn't like Jean, she recognized that Jean was probably just insensitive and showed bad judgement, rather than trying to get her fired. (This is a movement from Intentional/Hostile attribution to an Intrinsic one, which is lower on the scale.)

The practitioner met with Jean, who initially refused to apologize for anything. After discussing Sheri's view of the comments, Jean acknowledged that the comments could be seen as inappropriate, and agreed to apologize for writing them. She also wanted it clear that she wasn't trying to harm Anna, but only trying to improve her work.

The practitioner brought Anna and Jean together. Jean apologized for the comments, and Anna committed to civil and respectful interactions, along with not filing a formal complaint. Both agreed to meet with the supervisor and build ground rules, which they would ask the supervisor to monitor. Based on that, both agreed to go back to working together on a professional basis.

In an individual debrief with the practitioner, Anna stated that she didn't feel that Jean really understood how this had hurt her, but felt Jean had acknowledged enough for Anna to let it go and move forward. Jean, in her debrief, stated that she still felt Anna didn't like her, but if there was a reasonable and professional working relationship, that was enough for Jean to move forward.

— CHAPTER NINE —

MODEL #6:
THE DIMENSIONS OF CONFLICT

BACKGROUND OF THE DIMENSIONS MODEL

This model was derived from a recent book called *The Dynamics of Conflict Resolution*[1] by Bernard Mayer of CDR Associates. At the beginning of the book, Mayer proposes a set of concepts for understanding the "nature of conflict and the dynamics of how conflict unfolds."[2] This set of three concepts, as proposed and described by Mayer, form a useful and important model for understanding and working with the dynamics of conflict. This model also contains insightful ideas for framing and directing the scope of any interventions the practitioner may make in any given situation of conflict.

DIAGNOSIS WITH THE DIMENSIONS MODEL

The Dimensions of Conflict model is directed at understanding the dynamics of how conflict unfolds, and how it interacts on different levels. It allows the practitioner, when diagnosing a conflict, to assess the depth of three important "dimensions" that all conflicts bring to the table. While this model contains

1. Bernard Mayer, *The Dynamics of Conflict Resolution* (San Francisco: Jossey-Bass, 2000), 4.
2. Ibid, p. 4.

three elements in some ways similar to the Triangle of Satisfaction model, the dimensions that this model assesses are different and broader than the Triangle tool, which focuses more narrowly on specific types of interests. These three dimensions are not restricted to analyzing the parties' interests, but rather focus on deeper and broader areas relating to how we think about conflict, how we feel, and how we behave.

The Cognitive or Perceptual Dimension

This dimension looks at how the disputants think about and perceive conflict. Typically, parties carry beliefs and perceptions about themselves and the other party, and often reach conclusions or maintain assumptions that contribute to the conflict process. Frequently, for example, parties hold a belief that their own needs, wants, or values are incompatible with someone else's. This belief, whether true in an objective sense or not, frames and limits how the parties assess the situation, perhaps even preventing them from exploring solutions together. There are both objective and subjective parts to perception, and the various objective aspects often strengthen and reinforce the subjective perceptions and assumptions about the conflict situation, and vice versa. Objective perceptions of conflict often include the "facts," specific events, and other data. The subjective perceptions of the conflict include the beliefs the party carries, the conscious or unconscious assumptions the party makes in interpreting the facts or data, the attribution of motives and beliefs about the other party's intentions, selective memory of events, and the rewriting of history. In short, the cognitive dimension relates to how we think about and frame the conflict to ourselves and others.

Emotional Dimension

In addition to their thoughts and perceptions, people also react emotionally to conflict and overlay a wide range of feelings based on their perceptions. Indeed, feelings can be, and often are, independent of facts and objective perceptions (*I don't know why, but he just makes me angry!*). In conflict, even if we settle a dispute and agree to a resolution, we may still be carrying a large set of unresolved emotions about the conflict that has the potential to re-ignite the conflict in the future. We may not have found closure. From a conflict dynamic perspective, it is critical to assess the conflict from the emotional point of view to understand what emotions the parties are carrying in relation to the conflict, and how these emotions may affect the resolution process.

Behavioural Dimension

In addition to our perceptions about a conflict and our feelings about a conflict, we also make choices about what actions we will take, how we will behave in response to the conflict. This is the most overt and observable of the dimensions, and must be seen as being both interrelated with the other two dimensions and at the same time quite independent, requiring its own assessment. For example, strong feelings may result in very defensive behaviour in one person (or situation), or very aggressive behaviour in another, or very subdued, polite, avoidance behaviour in a third. In addition, one party's behaviour may be "triggering" another party leading to escalation, with the first party quite unaware how their behaviour is contributing to the problem. Conversely, one party may be triggering the other party quite deliberately, feeling that it's their only source of power in the situation. Overall, the behaviour of the parties is a key dimension that must be assessed and understood to help guide the practitioner's interventions.

In assessing or diagnosing a conflict, then, we can start by looking at all three dimensions of the conflict to better understand the dynamics involved. We can do this by simply working our way through the diagram as on the next page:

Dimensions Model: Diagnosis

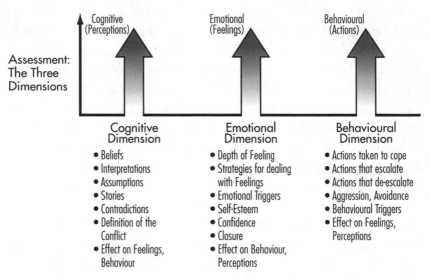

Assessment:
The Three
Dimensions

| Cognitive (Perceptions) | Emotional (Feelings) | Behavioural (Actions) |

Cognitive Dimension	Emotional Dimension	Behavioural Dimension
• Beliefs	• Depth of Feeling	• Actions taken to cope
• Interpretations	• Strategies for dealing	• Actions that escalate
• Assumptions	with Feelings	• Actions that de-escalate
• Stories	• Emotional Triggers	• Aggression, Avoidance
• Contradictions	• Self-Esteem	• Behavioural Triggers
• Definition of the	• Confidence	• Effect on Feelings,
Conflict	• Closure	Perceptions
• Effect on Feelings,	• Effect on Behaviour,	
Behaviour	Perceptions	

In diagnosing a situation, the model guides us to ask key questions about the conflict along the three dimensions.

Cognitive Dimension:

- How do the parties perceive or think about this conflict?
- What data are they focusing on? What are their conclusions about this data?
- What assumptions have they made and why?
- What is the tone and theme of the stories they tell about this conflict?
- How do they define this conflict?
- What motives have they attributed to the other party[3]? What data is there that contradicts this perception? How do they explain the contradictions?
- How are these perceptions affecting the thoughts, feelings, and behaviours of the other parties?
- What would change each party's view of the problem?

3. For an in-depth look at the process of attribution, refer to the Dynamics of Trust model.

Emotional Dimension:

• What are they feeling about the conflict?
• What is the depth of the feelings? How much venting is taking place or needed? How are they dealing with these feelings?
• How significant a barrier to resolution will these feelings be?
• What are the emotional "triggers" in place between the parties?
• What does this person need in order to release or let these feelings go?
• How are these feelings affecting the feelings, perceptions, and behaviours of the other parties?
• What would change how everyone felt about the problem?

Behavioural Dimension:

• What actions has each party taken to try to deal with the conflict?
• What behaviours are escalating the conflict?
• What behaviours are de-escalating the conflict?
• What behavioural "triggers" are in place between the parties?
• What is the risk of aggression or violence?
• What is the risk of withdrawal and avoidance?
• How are these behaviours affecting the actions, feelings, and perceptions of the other parties?
• What would change how everyone was behaving?

Once the practitioner has assessed the conflict along each of the three dimensions, she can begin to understand what dimensions are most strongly affecting the conflict, and begin to look at what interventions might be most helpful. Let's look at how the Dimensions model can be applied to our Case Study.

CASE STUDY: DIMENSIONS MODEL DIAGNOSIS

We'll go through the Case Study from the perspective of each of the Dimensions.

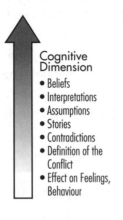

Cognitive
Dimension
• Beliefs
• Interpretations
• Assumptions
• Stories
• Contradictions
• Definition of the Conflict
• Effect on Feelings, Behaviour

Cognitive Dimension

Bob perceived the conflict as a situation where he was unfairly targeted, where his manager had created the new AS-1 position primarily as a way to punish or penalize him. Sally, however, perceived the situation as a common, routine one, where management was simply restructuring and changing the way services were delivered, and in no way was personally directed at Bob. Bob focused on the fact that Sally had developed a personal friendship with Diane as the reason he was treated unfairly. Sally focused on the fact that the job competition process was objective and fair, and therefore precluded any personal bias on her part. Cognitively, then, Bob saw this as an obvious personal attack (reinforced by Diane's aggressive behaviour), and Sally saw this as a simple restructuring of the department. Diane saw the problem as a management problem, not one that she could do anything about. The cognitive dimension for each of them was completely different.

The cognitive dimension was also having a direct effect on the other two dimensions. For Bob, the belief that Sally was targeting him made him fear for his job, and made him behave defiantly to (perhaps) show her he wasn't afraid. On the emotional dimension, the stress made Bob sick at times, and forced him to take numerous sick days.

Emotional Dimension

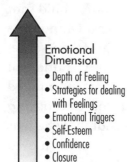

Emotional
Dimension

- Depth of Feeling
- Strategies for dealing
  with Feelings
- Emotional Triggers
- Self-Esteem
- Confidence
- Closure
- Effect on Behaviour,
  Perceptions

Feelings in this case were strong, especially on Bob's side. Bob identified feeling targeted and persecuted. He felt discriminated against because he was male. He felt that his last 12 years of work were being ignored, or worse, dismissed as worthless. Bob was 55 years old, whereas Diane was 34, which made him feel treated as old and no longer useful. Sally sensed how angry and defiant Bob was, which left her totally bewildered and not sure how to deal with his feelings. In addition, Sally was getting angry at Bob's "work-to-rule" behaviour, as she was beginning to lose face with the rest of the staff for letting Bob get away with it. Diane was also quite frustrated and helpless, in that she didn't feel any of this was her fault (since she couldn't do anything about any of it), but she was still forced to deal with Bob's moods. Bob was also personally angry and offended by Diane's yelling and swearing at him.

All of these feelings were making it harder and harder to find a solution. The high levels of emotion appeared to be triggering further negative behaviour and entrenching the parties' perceptions about each other.

Behavioural Dimension

Behavioural
Dimension

- Actions taken to cope
- Actions that escalate
- Actions that de-escalate
- Aggression, Avoidance
- Behavioural Triggers
- Effect on Feelings,
  Perceptions

The behavioural dimension was equally disparate. Bob responded to his feelings and perceptions of the problem by shutting down, by avoiding Sally and Diane as much as possible, and by simply not talking to either of them. His resistance and work-to-rule behaviour were his way of showing them how he felt. When Sally called a meeting with Bob, he showed up but would not explain his behaviour. This drove Sally crazy. Diane was equally frustrated with Bob. She would ask him to do something, and he wouldn't respond. When she'd "lose it" and yell at him, he withdrew even more. Sally, for her part, responded to this situation by constantly approaching Bob and asking what was going on, why he was doing this or that, how he was feeling, why, and so on. This was Sally's way of trying to resolve the situation. This behaviour upset Bob greatly, however, and increased his feeling of being singled out and targeted. Bob responded by taking large numbers of sick days, which presented a new problem for Sally, in that one of her objectives was to monitor and challenge sick days that were above average. When Sally questioned Bob's sick days, this reinforced his view that he was being targeted, and increased his negative behaviour.

Each party's behaviour seemed to be triggering more negative thoughts, feelings, and behaviour from the other parties.

As we can see, the situation is complex, but by breaking it into the three dimensions, the practitioner can begin to simplify the complexity and think about what interventions might help address one, two, or all three of the dimensions in the situation.

STRATEGIC DIRECTION FROM THE DIMENSIONS MODEL

The Dimensions model, like the others, gives a practitioner some direction on what might be done to help resolve the situation. For this, we ask the question, "For each of the three dimensions, what might help the parties move forward?"

To that end, the model directs the practitioner in the following way:

Dimensions Model: Strategic Guidance

	Cognitive Dimension	Emotional Dimension	Behavioural Dimension
Assessment: The Three Dimensions			
Strategic Direction: The Three Dimensions	• Look for New Data • Challenge the Interpretations • Uncover Assumptions • Build New Stories • Redefine the Conflict • Separate Intention from Impact • Ask, "What is needed to change the perception?"	• Acknowledge and validate the Feelings • Allow Venting • Remove Triggers • Build Confidence • Create Empowerment • Ask, "What is needed to change the feelings?"	• Remove Triggers • Identify Avoidance • Identify Aggression • Identify Behaviour that contributes to resolution • Build Ground Rules • Operationalize agreements • Ask, "What is needed to change damaging behaviours?"

Strategic Direction: Cognitive Dimension

From the cognitive perspective, some of the strategies the practitioner can use are:

- gathering data,
- questioning the interpretation of the information,
- understanding how the parties define the conflict,
- assessing the stories they are telling,
- identifying the assumptions they are making,
- identifying data that doesn't fit with their thinking about the situation.

By bringing out information that conflicts with the interpretation or assumptions of a party, the mediator can begin to shift the perceptions of the conflict held by the party.[4]

Additionally, based on the above, the practitioner can explore what each party would need to change their definition of the problem. This is an especially powerful approach, in that it draws out what is needed to achieve a significant change in how the problem is perceived. In many cases, when all parties

4. Refer to the process of "Attributional Retraining" in the Dynamics of Trust model.

have reflected and responded, the information given can form the basis for some "breakthrough" steps, steps that can dramatically alter the parties' perceptions of the conflict.

Strategic Direction: Emotional Dimension

Once the emotional dimension is diagnosed, the practitioner needs to help the parties to process or express that emotion constructively. This can be done by:

- listening,
- acknowledging,
- validating and legitimizing the feelings,
- allowing venting,
- building confidence,
- empowerment,
- removing "triggers,"
- reframing.

These skills and tools begin to help the parties deal with their emotions, minimize emotional barriers, and move on toward solutions and resolution.

In some cases, parties need to express their feelings to the other side and receive some sign that the other side heard them. The practitioner can then assess how to do this, and in what format it would be safe for all parties. In other cases, simply venting with the practitioner and working on new solutions is enough to move parties past the emotional barriers to resolution.

In many motor vehicle and personal injury cases, the plaintiff is looking for an apology. They have been injured, hurt, and it wasn't their fault. The insurance representatives often arrive interested only in talking about how much money the plaintiff wants to settle the legal claim. In these cases, a genuine apology or recognition of their injury, acknowledgement that this wasn't their fault, is needed before the monetary issues can be dealt with.

Strategic Direction: Behavioural Dimension

The first step, strategically, is to help the parties identify the outcomes of their behaviour, by:

- identifying aggression,
- identifying avoidance,
- identifying conciliatory gestures,
- identifying "triggers,"
- identifying any other behaviours that either escalate or de-escalate the conflict,
- building ground rules,
- operationalizing agreements.

By naming the behaviours that are contributing to the negative dynamic, or behaviours that are needed to move toward resolution, the practitioner is setting the stage for a constructive negotiation between the parties.

Jointly building ground rules between the parties can be extremely helpful. These ground rules or operating assumptions define and make explicit what behaviours will be acceptable to both parties. Having the parties then commit to the ground rules and agree to respectfully remind each other if any of the ground rules are not being followed, gives the parties an effective and constructive way of working together to improve each other's behaviour, an approach that will promote trust rather than blame.

"Operationalize" any solutions or agreements reached by taking specific situations the parties will face and have them work through (or even role-play) their behaviour in the situation. This gives the parties some actual experience in dealing with issues, so that when a problem arises in the future there is less chance they will revert to behaviour that caused the conflict in the first place. The practitioner can raise unexpected situations with the parties and ask them to work through how they'll handle them, ensuring it works for both. Out of this process, additional ground rules are often uncovered and added to the list.

Once the practitioner understands the behaviours that are both escalating the situation and helping resolve the situation, she can help the parties "bed-in" constructive behavioural changes in a way that resolves the behavioural dimension with the parties.

In one situation, a supervisor and manager were fighting constantly. The mediator explored the behavioural dimension and found that the supervisor responded to every suggestion the manager made with the phrase "But what won't work is this. . . . " The supervisor saw this as a way of raising problems to ensure that any solution would effectively solve those problems. The manager, however, interpreted this behaviour as resistance to solving the problem. After highlighting this behavioural trigger for both, the supervisor agreed to start his responses by first outlining what he liked about the suggestion, followed afterwards by his concerns. Once this change was bedded in, they found that a major part of their conflict disappeared.

CASE STUDY: DIMENSIONS MODEL STRATEGIC DIRECTION

Applying some of the strategic suggestions for intervention to our Case Study would look like this:

Cognitive
Dimension
• Look for New Data
• Challenge the Interpretation
• Uncover Assumptions
• Build New Stories
• Redefine the Conflict
• Separate Intention from Impact
• What is needed to change the perception?

Cognitive Dimension

Bob perceived the conflict as a situation where he was unfairly targeted, where Sally had created this new position primarily as a way to punish or penalize him. In speaking with Sally, the practitioner knew that this was not the case, as every department across the country was mandated to change to this new AS-1 "team lead" structure. The practitioner put this information to Bob, asking him to phone and verify it in the other centres. Bob verified this. Bob was then asked how this changed his perceptions of why the change was made here. Bob (grudgingly at first) conceded that maybe his assumptions about being targeted weren't completely accurate. The practitioner questioned him in the same way about the fairness of the job competition process by asking why the union felt the job competition process was reasonable. Bob conceded it was "probably" reasonable, but it wasn't how he would have structured it. The practitioner then asked Bob what he'd need to really change his view of Sally's intentions. Bob said he needed to see that she was prepared to help him get an AS-1 position by appointing him an "acting" AS-1 when Diane wasn't there. The practitioner asked Sally what she needed to see to change her perception that Bob was disrespectful and resistant. She answered that she wanted to see Bob at work with a positive attitude, taking ownership and initiative in the office, and needing to be "managed" less. She was especially keen to see a positive attitude in Bob, as that would signal that he had really turned around. She was prepared to consider him for "acting" assignments if she saw this kind of change. Bob responded that he was prepared to make some changes in his work style if she was prepared to appoint him.

The meeting, while difficult at times, went a long way in delivering what both said they needed in order to see the other person differently. The practitioner noted that addressing and changing the way both of them thought about and defined the conflict situation started to produce ideas and solutions.

Working on the cognitive dimension set the stage for a second joint meeting with Bob and Sally to begin finding a way to implement some of their ideas. This, in turn led to substantial changes in the cognitive dimension for both of them.

Behavioural Dimension

- Remove Triggers
- Identify Avoidance
- Identify Aggression
- Identify Behaviour that contributes to resolution
- Build Ground Rules
- Operationalize agreements
- What is needed to change damaging behaviours?

Behavioural Dimension

Since there were a number of behaviours that were problematic, the practitioner asked both Sally and Bob to describe the behaviours they didn't like, and to describe the impact the various behaviours had on them. As Sally and Bob described the behaviours that caused them problems, the practitioner noted and identified these behavioural "triggers" that were escalating the conflict. Together, Sally and Bob began defining what behaviour was acceptable and unacceptable for each of them. The practitioner also asked the parties what they would need in order to change some of these behaviours. Bob said that he was uncommunicative because he felt the manager was uncommunicative with him (demanding that everything go through Diane). What he needed was a commitment from Sally to include him in the information loop as a sign of good faith.[5] Sally had no problem with this as long as it primarily consisted of copying him in on the email and instructions she sent to Diane. They both agreed on this.

At a meeting between Bob and Diane, Bob stated that the yelling and swearing had to stop. Diane acknowledged this was wrong and would stop, but added that this happened because Bob didn't seem to respond when she spoke nicely. Bob said that since he and Sally had begun to resolve some larger issues, he would accept the tasks Diane asked him to do without a problem, assuming that she asked him respectfully. In addition, Bob agreed to respond politely when Diane needed a project update. Both committed to these behavioural changes.

---

5. This is a confidence building measure (CBM) – see the Dynamics of Trust model for more information on this.

Emotional Dimension

Emotional
Dimension
• Acknowledge and
  validate the Feelings
• Allow Venting
• Remove Triggers
• Build Confidence
• Create Empowerment
• What is needed to
  change the feelings?

Feelings, in this case, were strong. Bob started out the first caucus by saying that he'd never feel he could trust Sally because of her targeting him in this way. He even felt anger, mistrust, and frustration toward the union, who made it clear that they would not help him with this issue. After working through the cognitive issues and some behavioural issues, the parties tackled the emotional ones. The practitioner asked Bob if he wanted to feel like he was a valued employee and team member, to which Bob said yes. The same was confirmed for Sally. The practitioner asked them both what they'd need to begin feeling that way. Bob immediately said by being appointed acting team leader when Diane was away, he would feel that Sally trusted him. Sally immediately responded that her problem was that Bob didn't show any initiative in the job, and she needed to see that in order to justify the extra pay that the acting position received. Both agreed that Bob would demonstrate this initiative on two projects that needed someone to take the lead on, and if those went well, Bob would thereafter be eligible for the acting role. In addition, Sally stated that she needed to feel that Bob was coming to work with a positive, constructive attitude, and was contributing to the team without being asked. Bob stated that that was how he always came to work, at least until Sally took over the manager's job. He wanted to go back to that way, because he liked coming in to work happy. He stated that if the changes they had committed to behaviourally took place, he would feel that Sally was keeping her word, and he'd feel a lot better. Sally then looked directly at Bob and said she was very sorry for all the upset this whole situation had caused him. Bob, a bit surprised, thanked her for saying that.

Two months after the intervention, both parties reported feeling completely different (and significantly better) about their working relationship than they ever had previously.

ASSESSING AND APPLYING THE DIMENSIONS MODEL

Similar to the I/R/P model, the Dimensions model works with virtually all types of conflict, since the model assesses the three dimensions of the conflict process and does not attempt to categorize the conflict itself.

From a diagnostic point of view, then, the model is very strong, in that it can be applied to virtually any situation of conflict. The various substantive categories of conflict (commercial, family, community, workplace, etc.) all contain the dynamics represented by the Dimensions model in some fashion.

From a strategic point of view, the model gives clear and detailed guidance in each of the three Dimensions about types of interventions that may help. In addition, it shows clearly that each of the dimensions needs to be handled differently by using interventions appropriate to that dimension.

Final Thoughts on the Dimensions Model

A practitioner does not need to resolve all three dimensions in every case (although that is probably the ideal outcome). In some cases, all the parties want is a resolution on the behavioural dimension. For example, if two neighbours are fighting, they may only want to end the negative tit-for-tat behaviour of throwing garbage over each other's fence; they may not want to change their thinking about whose fault it is. If the behaviour were resolved, they could live contentedly by simply ignoring each other from then on. In other cases, the parties may only work on two out of three dimensions. For example, after resolving a lawsuit with a supplier, one company may want to understand why the other side behaved the way they did (cognitive dimension), and they may want the supplier to know how they feel the problem was handled (emotional dimension), but have no need of any behavioural resolution, since the two companies will never do business again.

There are many possibilities in the many situations of conflict we deal with in our life. What the Dimensions model helps with is assessing all three dimensions, and guiding the practitioner in choosing what dimensions need to be worked on and what kind of interventions are likely to help. This model can be applied in almost all situations.

PRACTITIONER'S WORKSHEET FOR THE DIMENSIONS MODEL

1. For this conflict, what is happening for each of these Dimensions?

Cognitive Dimension:	Emotional Dimension:	Behavioural Dimension:
• How do the parties perceive or think about this conflict?	• What are they feeling about the conflict?	• What actions has each party taken to try to deal with the conflict?
• What data are they focusing on? What are their conclusions about this data?	• What is the depth of the feelings? How much venting is taking place or needed? How are they dealing with these feelings?	• What behaviours are escalating the conflict?
• What assumptions have they made and why?		• What behaviours are de-escalating the conflict?
• What is the tone and theme of the stories they tell about this conflict?	• How significant a barrier to resolution will these feelings be?	• What behavioural "triggers" are in place between the parties?

(Continued)

• How do they define and think about this conflict? • What motives have they attributed to the other party? • How are these perceptions affecting the thoughts, feelings, and behaviours of the other parties? • What would change how each party is thinking about and framing the conflict?	• What are the emotional "triggers" in place between the parties? • How are these feelings affecting the feelings, perceptions, and behaviours of the other parties? • What would change how everyone felt about the problem?	• What is the risk of aggression or violence? • What is the risk of withdrawal and avoidance? • How are these behaviours affecting the actions, feelings, and perceptions of the other parties? • What would change how everyone was behaving?

2. What can the Practitioner focus on in each Dimension to help the parties?

Cognitive Strategies:	Emotional Strategies:	Behavioural Strategies:
• Look for new data • Challenge the interpretation • Uncover assumptions	• Acknowledge and validate the feelings • Allow venting • Remove triggers • Build confidence • Create empowerment	• Remove triggers • Identify avoidance • Identify aggression

• Look for data that challenges the assumptions • Build new stories • Redefine the conflict • Separate intention from impact • Explore, "What is needed to change the perception?" • Ask, "What would change each party's view of the problem?"	• Explore "What is needed to change the feelings?" • Ask, "What does this person need in order to release or let these feelings go?"	• Identify behaviour that contributes to resolution • Build ground rules • Operationalize agreements • Explore "What is needed to improve behaviours?" • Ask, "What does each person need to do differently?"

Interventions: **Choices:**	**Interventions:** **Choices:**	**Interventions:** **Choices:**

ADDITIONAL CASE STUDY: DIMENSIONS MODEL

Case Study: Who's the Gold Digger?

This was an estates case. A man, John, was elderly. His best friend, Peter, had helped him with his affairs for the last few years, but as John got older, he needed more and more care. Peter was a long-haul truck driver and couldn't provide all the care John needed. He suggested that John hire a nurse a few days a week.

Not long after, an old acquaintance of John's, named Nancy, called. Nancy and John had dated very briefly about 10 years before. She and John became close very quickly, and after a few months, she moved in and cared for John full time. Peter was very suspicious of Nancy, but she seemed committed to John and spent all her time with him attending to his needs. John paid her a little bit, but not much.

John deteriorated over the next year, and about 12 months after Nancy moved in, John passed away. There was some question about how lucid John was in the last few months. Right after his death, John's will was produced by his attorney in which he left the entire estate to Peter, since John didn't have any relatives or children. Peter was also named the executor. The estate was valued at about $500,000. Before Peter could do anything, Nancy produced two later wills, one clearly signed by John and properly witnessed, dated about six months before his death. In this will, the estate was equally divided between Peter and Nancy, with Peter still named as executor. The other will was from one month before his death, was clearly signed by John but not witnessed by anyone, and in this will, the entire estate was left to Nancy, with Nancy named as executor. Nancy asserted that she was entitled to the entire estate.

Lawsuits were filed, but given the uncertainty of the wills, lawyers for both parties decided to try mediation. At the mediation, both Peter and Nancy were upset and angry at each other, so much so that the mediator took them into caucus early.

In caucus, Peter exploded. He called Nancy nothing but a gold digger, someone who had preyed on his friend John just for the money, and he refused to allow her to have a penny. He swore that he'd never give in to such a con artist, a fraud artist, a conniving woman who had sucked his friend dry. She was immoral and evil, in Peter's eyes. On top of that, he couldn't stand it when Nancy referred to John as "John-boy," which had been Peter's nickname for John. Peter said he didn't care about the money; he couldn't allow her to get away with this.

Both lawyers agreed that the last will was probably not valid. Both lawyers also agreed that the second-last will had a strong chance of being accepted, since there was no evidence of mental infirmity in John at that time. That meant that the estate would most likely be split between Nancy and Peter.

Dimensions Model Diagnosis and Worksheet: Who's the Gold Digger?

Cognitive Dimension:	Emotional Dimension:	Behavioural Dimension:
• Peter saw Nancy as immoral and dishonest. • Peter saw Nancy as taking advantage of an old man, something he saw as despicable.	• Peter carried a huge level of emotion over this situation and had frequent angry outbursts. • Peter was probably still grieving the loss of his friend, which amplified his anger in this situation of conflict.	• Peter refused to settle, would not agree to sign any money over to Nancy. • Peter was triggered every time Nancy used Peter's nickname for John, something Peter saw as "his," something deeply personal that she had stolen.

It was clear that all three dimensions were at work here, with the cognitive and the emotional the strongest. Even Peter's lawyer couldn't get through to Peter to listen to some possible alternatives. Nancy was willing to accept something like a splitting of the assets, but Peter would not hear of it.

The mediator, based on the above diagnosis with the Dimensions model, could use interventions described on the pages that follow.

Dimensions Model Strategic Direction: Who's the Gold Digger?

Emotional Dimension

This was in some ways very straightforward—Peter was angry and hurt, both by John's death and by what he perceived as Nancy trying to steal John's money.

The mediator, in caucus, simply asked how Peter felt, and listened to him vent for close to an hour, asked him about John, what he was like, what his values were, etc. This allowed Peter to vent some of his anger, to really get it off his chest. This had the effect of helping Peter to process some of his emotions, process some of the anger, to allow him to move on a bit.[6]

At that point, the mediator shifted to the Cognitive Dimension.

Cognitive Dimension

On the Cognitive Dimension, the mediator assessed that Peter would refuse to negotiate at all until his view of the conflict changed in some significant ways. For this reason, the mediator focused on:

- Challenging Peter's assumptions, and
- Separating intention from impact

---

6. For more help in the grieving process, see the Moving Beyond model

To challenge the assumptions, the mediator talked at length with Peter, asking him about John, John's life, and what it was like near the end. Peter explained that John had gotten more and more lonely over the last few years, and would often talk about his fear of dying alone. Peter stated this was why Nancy had been able to take advantage of John.

The mediator asked Peter whether Peter's view of Nancy would change if Nancy had been with John for 10 years, taking care of him as he got less and less functional and always being with John. Then Peter thought about it, and said sure— if she had been there that long, she would have proven that she wasn't just after the money. The mediator asked Peter if he was happy that John had had companionship for the last year of his life, if the fact that John didn't die alone was a good thing. Again, Peter stopped and thought, and grudgingly admitted that there was no way that he could have spent that amount of time with John. He also admitted that John had appeared happy.

The mediator then separated intention from impact, but in this case in a reverse sort of way. The mediator asked Peter to assume that Nancy was just out for the money, to assume that her intention was to spend so much quality time with John that he'd change his will. Peter had no problem with this assumption. The mediator then asked, "If this lousy intention had the impact of giving John happiness and companionship during the last year of his life, regardless of the intention, was that a valuable and good thing for John?" Peter again stopped, thought, and admitted that that was very valuable to John. The mediator then asked, "Do you think John would feel that was important enough to him that he'd want Nancy getting something fair from his estate?" After a long pause, Peter conceded that John would probably want Nancy to get something.

Finally, the mediator talked to Peter about how he viewed his role in this process. Peter emphatically stated that his role was to make sure that John's memory was not clouded or muddied by Nancy. The mediator asked what John would think about his hard-earned money being spent on lawyers and court trying to prevent Nancy from getting some money that John would probably want her to have. At this point Peter simply asked, "Well, how much does she want?"

This question signaled a cognitive shift for Peter from "I won't let her have a penny," to "She's going to get something. Let's talk about how much."

Behavioural Dimension

At this point, the mediator focused on the behavioural side, suggesting that the feelings were too strong for the parties to meet together (especially because whenever Nancy referred to John, she used his nickname John-boy, which triggered Peter's anger), but that they begin negotiating some fair numbers. Counsel got much more involved, and after a few rounds of offers, a number just less than half the estate was agreed to be paid to Nancy.

Epilogue of the Case Study

By the end of the meeting, Peter said goodbye to Nancy, and while he still carried the belief that she had in some ways tried to take advantage of John, he also saw that she had treated him well in his last year and was willing to recognize that. The case settled.

— CHAPTER TEN —

MODEL #7:
THE SOCIAL STYLE MODEL

BACKGROUND OF THE SOCIAL STYLE[1] MODEL

One of the most common framings of conflict is the ubiquitous "personality conflict." Personality conflicts seem to abound, yet there is very little consistency or common understanding about what personality conflict is, or what should be done about it. There are a wide variety of models that attempt to assess different personality traits and give guidance on what can be done about the different personalities that are encountered in the world. Most of these models tend to be focused around the idea of communication styles.

Communications, and the quality of our communication processes, are central to the experience of conflict. For conflict practitioners, therefore, having a workable model to assist with personality and communication issues is important.

The most commonly known and referenced system for assessing personality traits is the Myers-Briggs Personality Type Indicator (MBTI)[2]. Much has been written on the Myers-Briggs model; hundreds of thousands of people have taken the

---

1. Social Style is copyrighted material owned by The TRACOM Group and used here with permission.
2. I.B. Myers and M.H. McCaulley, *A Guide to the Development and Use of the Myers-Briggs Type Indicator* (Palo Alto, CA: Consulting Psychologists Press, 1985).

MBTI assessment, creating a large database of statistical trends and analysis.

There is one significant drawback to using the MBTI system as a conflict practitioner, however: the MBTI model is based on how a person internally approaches processing and communicating information, and these internal processes are extremely hard to observe. The most common way MBTI is used is to have individuals fill out the MBTI assessment tool (a form of questionnaire) that assesses and categorizes the individual's personality and information processing traits. The results from this assessment are then made available to the individual or the work group. This means that to be useful in a conflict situation the mediator or practitioner would need to ask parties to fill out the MBTI questionnaire before the intervention; while that is not out of the question, it severely limits the usefulness of the model.

In looking for an individual style-based analysis model, therefore, a more effective tool would be a model that assessed personality based on observable behaviour, not internal processes. The Social Style Model fits this requirement.

The Social Style Model[3] is another style model that comes from the same roots as the Myers-Briggs Personality Type Indicator, with two significant differences. First, the Social Style approach is focused on an individual's observable behaviour, not internal processes. This means that observable behaviour can help the practitioner assess the predominant "style" of the people in the dispute, and can make intervention decisions based on that assessment. Formal instruments and questionnaires do exist for assessing behavioural style under the Social Style Model, with one significant difference; since observable behaviour is the basis of the model, the Social Style assessment relies more on peer assessment and less on individual self-assessment. In addition, the formal use of questionnaires, whether self or peer, is not required to make effective use of the

---

3. D. W. Merrill and R. H. Reid, *Personal Styles & Effective Performance*, (CRC Press: Boca Raton, 1984).

Social Style Model; it can be useful to a practitioner by simply observing the behaviour of the parties.

Secondly, the Social Style Model is much simpler. The Social Style Model relies on and assesses two dimensions of behaviour, assertiveness and emotional responsiveness. This produces four possible "styles" or types; by comparison, the MBTI works with four different dimensions of internal processes which produces 16 different types, a far more complex and difficult model to work with. So Social Style, therefore, is more functional and effective in the conflict and dispute resolution field.

DIAGNOSIS WITH THE SOCIAL STYLE MODEL

In terms of the diagnostic assessment with the Social Style Model, the first step is to identify the styles of the people involved. This requires direct observation of the parties' behaviour (as opposed to inferring the inner qualities of the people involved). This is done by looking for indicators along two broad dimensions of human behaviour, assertiveness and responsiveness.

Assertiveness is defined as "the degree to which others perceive a person as tending to ask or tell in interactions with others." People who are more reserved, tentative, and who tend to keep their thoughts to themselves are "ask" assertive, whereas those who are more forceful and direct in their interactions are "tell" assertive. The model recognizes that people, in general, try to get what they want, and this dimension measures how they do this as either more "ask" assertive or more "tell" assertive.

Responsiveness is defined as "the degree to which others perceive a person as tending to control or display emotions when interacting. Individuals who are more controlled do not typically display much emotion when interacting. They tend to be concerned with getting things done in a no-nonsense manner, and tend to be more distant and formal. Those people with an emoting disposition display their emotions more to others, and are characterized by their relatively casual manner. These individuals like to get involved with others on a personal basis.

Both dimensions have specific, observable behaviours that give clear indicators of where the person fits on the particular scale.

Indicators of Assertiveness

Ask Assertive ⟵	**Behaviour** ⟶	Tell Assertive
Less	**Amount of Talking**	More
Slower	**Rate of Speaking**	Faster
Softer	**Voice Volume**	Louder
Less, Slower	**Body Movement**	More, Faster
Indirect	**Eye Contact**	Direct
Leans Back	**Posture**	Leans Forward
Less	**Forcefulness of Gestures**	More

Tell assertive individuals tend to talk more, talk louder, speak at a faster pace, tend to move faster, lean forward, and use forceful gestures. Overall, they tend to demonstrate higher energy. Ask assertive people tend to speak less often, slower and softer, they move slower, lean back, and gesture with less emphasis, if they gesture at all.

Indicators of Responsiveness

Control Responsive ⟵	**Behaviour** ⟶	Emote Responsive
Controlled	**Facial Animation**	Animated
Monotone	**Vocal Animation and Variance**	Inflection
Restrained, few gestures or facial expressions	**Physical Animation**	Animated, strong use of physical gestures, such as hands and face expressions

Control Responsive ←	**Behaviour** →	Emote Responsive
Rigid	**Body Posture**	Casual
Tasks	**Subjects of Speech**	People
Facts & Data	**Type of Descriptives**	Opinions & Stories
Less	**Use of Hands**	More

Emote responsive people are more animated physically and facially and use smooth, flowing gestures. They show their own feelings and acknowledge other people's feelings more often. Control responsive people[4] are less animated, they gesture less, and don't tend to acknowledge their own or other people's feelings.

The Four Social Styles
Once the practitioner has assessed the parties from the assertiveness and responsiveness indicators, he can set the two dimensions together on a grid. This produces four quadrants or "styles" of behaviour, as shown here.

Social Style Model: Diagnosis

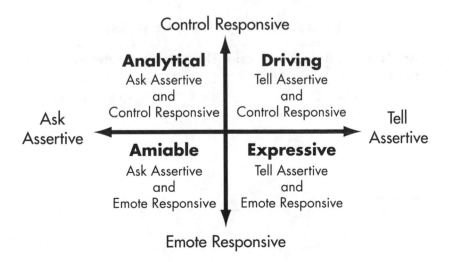

---

4. It should be noted that in regard to responsiveness, control responsive people have just as many feelings as anyone else, and there is no implication otherwise. The only distinction is whether they allow those feelings to show or not.

Analytical Style: Analytical Style people are more ask assertive than 50 percent of the population, and more control responsive than 50 percent of the population.

Driving Style: Driving Style people are more tell assertive than 50 percent of the population, and more control responsive than 50 percent of the population.

Expressive Style: Expressive Style people are more tell assertive than 50 percent of the population, and more emote responsive than 50 percent of the population.

Amiable Style: Amiable Style people are more ask assertive than 50 percent of the population, and more emote responsive than 50 percent of the population.

Based on the dimensions of assertiveness and responsiveness, and on the characteristics and interrelationships of these dimensions, the four Social Style groups have different qualities and tendencies identified in the following ways:

Characteristics of the Four Styles

Analytical Characteristics:	**Driving Characteristics:**
Prudent	Independent
Task-Oriented	Task- and Results-Oriented
Detail-Focused	Decisive
Slow, Careful Decision Makers	Fast-Paced
Logical	Dominating
Low-Key	

Amiable Characteristics:	Expressive Characteristics:
Dependable	Visionary
Relationship-Oriented	Animated
Supportive	Flamboyant
Confrontation-Averse	High-energy, fast-paced
Open	Impulsive
Pliable	Opinionated

Once the practitioner understands the predominant style of the people involved and locates them in one of the quadrants, he or she can then begin assessing the problems or causes of the conflict.

The Social Style Model focuses on communication problems that can result from a clash of the above styles. It shows that conflict is frequently caused by a mismatch in the styles themselves, not solely from the content of the problem. For example, if two individuals are working together on a project, one with a Driving style and the other an Amiable style, some of the key style differences may clash. The Driving style may be strongly task-focused and quick to make decisions to move the project ahead, regardless of any feathers that might get ruffled. The Amiable style, on the other hand, may balk at the decisions proposed, wanting to get buy-in from the people affected first, since Amiables tend to be focused on the relationships involved to a much greater degree than the Driving. This may create and escalate a workplace conflict, regardless of the actual project decisions or outcomes themselves.

The Social Style Model is also based on the assumption that personal styles are unconsciously learned, meaning that as we learn and grow we get comfortable with our predominant style, and we do this without choosing it. It simply becomes a core part of how we conduct ourselves. It is also based on the assumption that our predominant style is substantially permanent. This means that our "personality," our core behavioural style, is unlikely to change. In some ways our style is like our native language: it is typically our most comfortable means to communicate even if we learn other languages during our life.

Let's take a look at how the Social Style Model can help in conflict situations.

CASE STUDY: SOCIAL STYLE DIAGNOSIS

In looking at our Case Study, the first step will be to assess the Social Style of the people involved. Below is a description and assessment of the three parties.

- **Bob:** Bob was a very quiet, soft-spoken man who gravitated to very detail-oriented tasks such as accounting and record keeping. He spoke slowly, thought carefully before answering, and appeared very even-tempered and low-key. He spoke in a very quiet monotone with little expression, and tended to look down when he spoke, moving little. Even when angry, Bob's expression was virtually unchanged. Based on the above observations, he is ask assertive and control responsive, placing him as a strong Analytical.

- **Sally:** Sally was a high-energy individual who loved to describe the "big picture," where she was leading the department, and how excited she was about the benefits of that. She spoke quickly, used her hands when she spoke, and often drew pictures on a flip chart to illustrate her point. While not particularly argumentative, she often revisited points of disagreement to insist that her assessment made sense. She leaned forward when she spoke, and often waited for the other person's reaction to what she said to confirm that they "got" her point, only then moving on to the next point. She was easy to "read" in terms of how she felt, and tended to be positive and upbeat in general. She scored as emote responsive and tell assertive, placing her solidly in the Expressive category.

- **Diane:** Diane was also quiet, but focused and to the point. She didn't speak very much, but when she did it was firm and clear. She made her points succinctly, and expected a quick response to them. Her sentences were short and very action focused, such as "Please do this," or "That's fine, do it." She spoke little about how she felt, and focused on the task at hand. She didn't like beating around the bush, and would rather do the task than talk about it. She didn't understand why people couldn't simply get the job done and move on. She rated as tell assertive and control responsive, placing her in the Driving style.

Based on the above assessment, it became clear that one aspect of the conflict was a significant communication problem. Bob complained that Sally never listened, talked over him and interrupted him, and didn't give him time to express himself. Sally complained that Bob didn't respond at all, that she would ask him a question and he would sit there and just stare at her. She would then continue talking, since he didn't seem to be willing to. A significant part of the problem was their communication patterns and personal styles.

Between Bob and Diane, the problems were fewer, but still there. Diane found Bob to be slow and almost incapable of making decisions. Diane would ask him to do something; he seemed to agree, and then days later he would raise some well-thought-out objections, thus delaying the task far too long. Bob found Diane to be pushy and demanding, and often rash in her decisions. He felt he was acting responsibly by raising problems before pressing forward and doing the task and didn't understand why this upset her. On the other hand, both Bob and Diane were detail oriented and liked the feeling of finishing tasks and projects, and on that front they worked well together.

As the analysis above shows, both relationships suffered from a poor communication process caused by a significant difference in styles, or what we often refer to as "personality." A practitioner diagnosing the conflict from this perspective can learn some effective interventions from the Social Style Model.

STRATEGIC DIRECTION FROM THE SOCIAL STYLE MODEL

Strategically, the Social Style Model suggests three important interventions once the diagnosis is complete:

1. Be versatile and flexible—change your style toward the other person's style to make them more comfortable,

2. Translate the communication of one party into your style (or the style of another party as appropriate), and

3. When functioning as a third party, coach each person on how to change their style when they communicate with people of different styles, where appropriate.

Versatility—Working Well With All Styles

A core concept in intervening using this model is the idea of "versatility." It is by being flexible in our behaviour that we can improve communications, and the Social Style Model offers two ideas to improve our versatility:

• First, we can all use behaviours from all four styles in different situations and circumstances. Human beings do not fit neatly into simple boxes and stay there. We respond in a variety of ways to the situations we encounter, and we use a range of styles and skills.

- Secondly, everyone has a favourite or predominant style that they spend a lot of time using, a style that they are most comfortable with. This is their "home base," the style in which they will best hear and understand other people's communications.

To go back to our analogy of language, our predominant style is our native tongue, the one we are most comfortable with. That said, many people become fluent in second and third languages, which greatly expands their ability to communicate in the world. When two people meet, one who speaks three languages and one only their native language, it makes sense for both to speak the common language rather than each insisting on speaking their own native tongue. In other words, one person needs to do something for the other person and agree to speak the other's language in order to facilitate their communication. The idea behind being versatile is that the other party will be able to hear and understand the communication better if the content is presented in a style that is similar to their own style.

In situations where a problem is arising not necessarily because of the content itself, but because the content is getting lost or distorted due to a personality problem or a style conflict, we can change our communication style and choose behaviours that will make others more comfortable. We can choose to do something for others in order to be better heard and received.

This idea of versatility or "doing something for others" is already implicit in our society and culture to a great degree, and should not be seen as a new or foreign concept. For example, when talking to someone who has just learned English recently, we tend to slow down, speak a bit clearer, and perhaps choose language that will be easier for a new speaker of the language to understand. When we are speaking to a non-technical person about a technical issue, we will tend to adapt the way we communicate to make it clearer for the other person by using less technical jargon. In the same way, if we are an Expressive and we know the other person is an Analytical, we should do some flexing of our message into a style that an Analytical can best hear and understand it; in addition, we should decode what the Analytical is saying to better understand it from an Expressive's point of view.

Social Style Model: Strategic Guidance

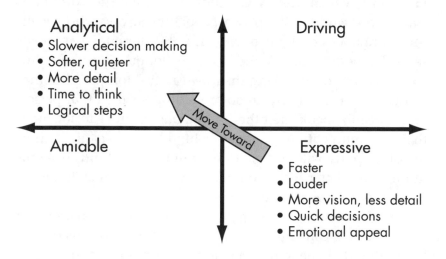

So what exactly is versatility? As the strategic guidance figure shows, shifting from Expressive behaviours to Analytical behaviours would entail choices like speaking slower and quieter, using more hard data or information, presenting logical steps rather than emotional appeals, paying attention to details, and giving the Analytical a bit more time to process the information and come back later with questions. The net result of these behavioural changes is that the speaker's message is clearly delivered, eliminating resistance and conflict caused by the communication style or personality getting in the way.

Style versatility is primarily a behavioural change, and the following four behaviours are the most important to adjust, as appropriate to the circumstances.

Adjust your style in stages:

- Pace: Faster or Slower
- Detail/Structure: More or Less
- Small talk: More or Less
- Focus: Facts or Feelings

For all four styles, a brief indicator of the type of versatility choices that might help follows.

Amiables Working With:

Analyticals:	Drivers:
• Be more task-oriented • De-emphasize feelings • Be systematic • Be well organized, detailed, and structured • Less small talk	• Pick up the pace • Demonstrate higher energy • Be more task-oriented • De-emphasize feelings • Be clear about goals and plans • Cut to the chase
Amiables:	Expressives:
• Be careful not to over-emphasize Amiable tendencies • Introduce some aspects of other styles to balance the style that is predominant	• Pick up the pace • Demonstrate higher energy, • Focus on the Big Picture • Say what you think – be candid and direct • Facilitate their self-determination

Drivers Working With:

Analyticals:	Drivers:
• Slow your pace down • Listen more, listen better • Don't come on too strong • Be prepared to listen to more than you want to know • Recognize details as important	• Be careful not to over-emphasize Driving tendencies • Introduce some aspects of other styles to balance the style that is predominant
Amiables:	**Expressives:**
• Make genuine personal contact, more warmth • Slow your pace down • Phrase ideas provisionally • Focus more on feelings • Be supportive and empathetic • Provide structure • Demonstrate interest in the human side of the issues	• Make personal contact, more warmth • Focus more on feelings • Cooperate with conversational spontaneity • Be open to some "fun" in the process • Give them recognition for their contribution • Provide considerable freedom • Acknowledge the Big Picture

Expressives Working With:

Analyticals:	Drivers:
• Slow your pace down • Listen more, listen better • Don't come on too strong • Be task-oriented and systematic • De-emphasize feelings • More detail • Give them time to make decisions	• Be more task-oriented • De-emphasize feelings • Plan your work and work your plan • Be organized in your communications • Avoid power struggles • Less small talk
Amiables:	**Expressives:**
• Listen more, listen better • Open with some small talk • Slow your pace down • Decrease your intensity • Don't interrupt • Be supportive and empathetic • Focus on logic and data • Pay attention to details • Acknowledge importance of relationships	• Be careful not to overemphasize Expressive tendencies • Introduce some aspects of other styles to balance the style that is predominant

Analyticals Working With:

Analyticals:	Drivers:
• Be careful not to over-emphasize Analytical tendencies • Introduce some aspects of other styles to balance the style that is predominant	• Pick up the pace • Demonstrate higher ener-gy • Don't get bogged down in details or theory • Say what you think • Speak in results-oriented terms • Allow them to be self-directed
Amiables:	Expressives:
• Make genuine personal contact, small talk • Focus more on feelings • Offer to lend a hand • Provide structure • Don't overdo facts and logic • Pay attention to relation-ships	• Make personal contact • Pick up the pace • Demonstrate higher energy • Focus more on feelings • Cooperate with conversa-tional spontaneity • Allow for some "fun" • Say what you think • Recognize the Expressive's work • Acknowledge the Big Picture

By becoming skilled and versatile, the practitioner can greatly reduce resistance and friction in the communication system.

Translating and Coaching the Social Style Model

Another way a practitioner can help parties in a conflict is to assist by translating one person's communication from their predominant style into the other person's predominant style, using a variety of skills and tools such as restating, reframing, paraphrasing, or changing the pacing, tone, and intensity. In this case, translating involves a great degree of versatility on the part of the translator, in that they need to reach out across a whole range of styles from the speaker's style to the receiver's style, both of which may be different from the translator's style.

In mediation, for example, when all parties are present, it may be necessary to translate one party's style into a style that helps the other party to hear and understand. In one case, a strong Analytical lawyer began a joint session with a long explanation about what they liked and didn't like about the other party's last offer. Opposing counsel was a Driving style, and was getting visibly more and more agitated the longer the Analytical spoke. The mediator gently intervened, asking, "At the end of the day, what are you recommending about their last offer?" The Analytical, looking surprised, said, "Well, we're accepting it, of course, but I thought you needed to know why." The Driver stood up, offered his hand, and said, "All I need is a signed agreement." The Analytical, in this case, had almost blown an agreement by staying stuck in his own style.

In regards to coaching, the practitioner may be in the position of helping one party adapt their behaviour to be better heard by the other side. In many negotiations or mediations, the practitioner will have each party describe and explain their issues directly to the other party. In caucus, the practitioner may well coach or prep one party to modify their presentation to make it more effective. For example, if a Driver is presenting to an Amiable, they may need to address the relationship issues (something a Driving style may simply not think of), rather than just focus on the money or the task.

CASE STUDY: SOCIAL STYLE STRATEGIC DIRECTION

In our Case Study, there would need to be two interventions, one between Sally and Bob, and a second between Bob and Diane.

Sally and Bob

In this meeting, there needs to be a significant amount of versatility taking place. Because of her role as the manager, as well as the fact that Bob appeared less flexible than Sally, the mediator focused on helping Sally do the majority of the style adapting. Prior to the meeting, the mediator met with Sally and shared the concept of versatility with her. She stated she was willing to try, if it would help. The mediator coached Sally to slow down, focus on data and logic, give Bob time to digest and think about what was said, and not force quick decisions. In addition, the mediator coached Bob to ask for time to think rather than just go silent. During the meeting, the mediator helped both parties translate back and forth from the Analytical to the Expressive when needed. The result was a very productive meeting at which Bob heard and considered some key information for the first time (the fact that the structural changes were nationwide, for example, and the reasons why seniority wasn't considered in the promotion), and Sally heard how hard it was for Bob to feel like his last 12 years didn't count for anything when he had helped manage so much of the paperwork in that office. This greatly improved their ability to hear each other, and allowed them to focus on solving each other's problem, the first time they had ever reached that point. Bob even surprised Sally by saying he didn't need time to go away think about the discussion; he was prepared to stand by the decisions they made today. After the meeting, both Sally and Bob spoke to the mediator and wondered what had made the "other person change so much."

Diane and Bob

A very similar process, except that the mediator decided that neither would benefit from coaching ahead of time and spent most of the meeting translating between the Driver (Diane) and the Analytical (Bob). The main point of contention in their communication process was how work would be assigned, followed up, and completed. Diane, a Driving style, was most comfortable telling Bob what to do and giving him orders. As an Analytical, Bob wanted time to root around the problem before agreeing to the decision. In the end both parties made changes for the other, Bob accepting orders on the simple and obvious tasks, and Diane accepting that Bob would need time to think about and raise issues on the more complex tasks. Since both were task-oriented, they quickly agreed to develop a written description detailing exactly how various situations would be handled between them.

In both cases above, the practitioner followed the strategic direction of the model:

1. The mediator adapted his style toward each of the other parties' styles when communicating with them.
2. The mediator translated the communications of one party into the style of the other party.
3. The mediator coached Sally and Bob on how to change their style when they communicated with each other.

ASSESSING AND APPLYING THE SOCIAL STYLE MODEL

The Social Style Model is broadly applicable to many conflicts in that it applies to the personality and communication part of the conflict process. It is not as directly helpful in other aspects of conflict where structural or substantive issues are the main barriers, as the model doesn't work directly with the content of any given situation.

Diagnostically, the model is valid though somewhat limited in its range of use since it only diagnoses conflict that is generated from communications problems. This ranks it only a medium on the diagnostic scale.

Strategically, the model directs a practitioner to make simple changes to his or her communication patterns to help with the personality and communication issues. It ranks medium to high on the strategic scale.

Final Thoughts on the Social Style Model

Overall, the Social Style Model ranks high in importance, in that all practitioners need a framework for addressing personality and communication conflicts in order to be effective when working with a wide range of clients. The whole area of personality conflict and communication issues within conflict is complex and detailed, making personality-related conflict one of the hardest areas to address. The Social Style Model is one of the simplest and most effective models for tackling this, and therefore is one of the most important tools a practitioner can have.

PRACTITIONER'S WORKSHEET FOR THE SOCIAL STYLE MODEL

1. Assess the individuals along both dimensions, Assertiveness and Responsiveness.

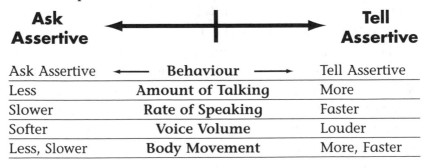

Ask **Assertive**		**Tell** **Assertive**
Ask Assertive ⟵	**Behaviour** ⟶	Tell Assertive
Less	**Amount of Talking**	More
Slower	**Rate of Speaking**	Faster
Softer	**Voice Volume**	Louder
Less, Slower	**Body Movement**	More, Faster

	Eye Contact	
Indirect		Direct
Leans Back	**Posture**	Leans Forward
Less	**Forcefulness of Gestures**	More

Control
Responsive ← → **Emote**
Responsive

Control Responsive ←	**Behaviour**	→ Emote Responsive
Controlled	**Facial Animation**	Animated
Monotone	**Vocal Animation** **and Variance**	Inflection
Restrained, few gestures or facial expressions	**Physical Animation**	Animated, strong use of physical gestures, such as hands and face expressions
Rigid	**Body Posture**	Casual
Tasks	**Subjects of Speech**	People
Facts & Data	**Type of Descriptives**	Opinions & Stories
Less	**Use of Hands**	More

2. Place the individuals into a quadrant on the grid.

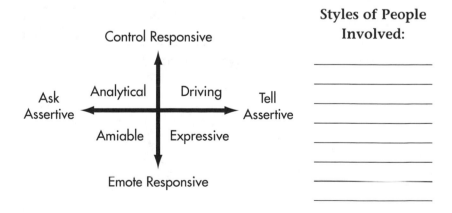

Styles of People
Involved:

_____

_____

_____

_____

_____

_____

_____

3. Assess what strategies will help, and where they should be applied.

Where will versatility help? What steps can be taken to adapt to other styles?

Pace:	Faster or Slower?
Detail and Structure:	More or Less?
Small Talk:	More or Less?
Focus	More on Facts? More on Feelings?

Where will translating help? Between which parties?

Where will coaching help? Which parties?

ADDITIONAL CASE STUDY: SOCIAL STYLE MODEL

Case Study: The Vision Thing

A small start-up company was experiencing a significant amount of conflict. The company had 35 staff, including five supervisors, two directors, and the CEO. In the two years they'd been functioning the company had been very successful, and the CEO was committed to an "open" management style. He met with the entire staff twice a year, each time sharing the status of the company in relation to the business plan, how the company was doing, and painted a clear picture and vision for where the company was going. The company delivered services in a very technical area of a financial services field.

About six months after the initial staff were hired, there was some grumbling about not being able to trust the CEO and concern about the direction of the company. Initially the CEO ignored the grumbling, but it continued to grow. The CEO asked his management team to communicate more with the staff, to reiterate the vision and direction, but it seemed to get worse. The CEO arranged another town hall, once again articulated the direction and goals of the company, and again thought that he had gotten through to the staff. The dissent, however, continued to grow and became a significant drain on morale in the company. The CEO didn't know what to do, but continued meeting with the staff as much as possible to reassure them and talk about the future of the company. The downward spiral, however, continued.

To try to turn things around, the CEO once again held a town hall meeting, trying to rally the staff and get them refocused on the future and the goals of the company. It didn't help. Three staff members quit to take other positions, and there was a widespread feeling that this was no longer a good place to work.

Social Style Model Diagnosis: The Vision Thing

The management team decided to do a large-scale intervention, and brought in consultants who recommended the use of the Social Style instrument. Everyone in the company was assessed by three peers, right up to and including the CEO. The results were startling. Of the 35 staff, the styles broke down this way:

- Amiables – 2
- Drivers – 5
- Analyticals – 27
- Expressives – 1

Even more interesting were the roles held by the different styles. Of the five supervisors, three were Drivers and two were Analyticals. Of the two directors, one was Amiable, the other a Driver. And the lone Expressive was the CEO.

This information was shared at a full company retreat, immediately revealing a major source of the dissatisfaction and conflict. It became clear that what was missing was not communication in general (as there was lots of that) but rather a specific type of communication. The Analyticals were missing a significant amount of detail and structure about the company plans and directions, information that Analyticals typically need to feel comfortable and well informed. The CEO had correctly sensed that more communication was needed, but what he gave them was a broad vision for the future (something that Expressives focus on) rather than specific detail (that Analyticals need). This had the effect of convincing the Analyticals that the CEO didn't really know what he was doing, that he was blowing smoke rather than giving them concrete information about the short-term, tactical steps that would actually help achieve the vision. The more the CEO gave them the "big picture" rather than the tactics and details, the less they trusted him.

In addition, three of the supervisors were Drivers who had little patience for the type of information and decision-making time the Analyticals needed. When they asked for input from their teams, they rarely gave the people enough time to give thoughtful responses, and consequently at least three of the teams felt railroaded by their supervisors.

It became clear that the style and quality of communication needed to be improved.

Social Style Model Strategic Direction: The Vision Thing

The consultants asked the CEO these questions as to what should be done strategically to resolve the issues:

Where will versatility help? What steps can be taken to adapt to other styles?

The CEO clearly needed to increase his versatility, and he made a commitment to doing this. He met with various teams, asked for input on what kind of information they needed, and gave them time to consider and respond.

He found very quickly that what many in the company needed, in addition to the vision and direction, were tangible goals and specific steps aimed at the short term. In essence, most staff wanted guidance on "What do I do Monday morning?"

The management team made immediate plans to change how the company communicated and tailored it to the Analytical style, without completely ignoring the needs of the other styles.

Where will translating help? Between which parties?

Given the difference in styles in the company along with the preponderance of Analyticals, a committee was struck that was weighted with Analytical staff with the goal of monitoring the needs of staff on an ongoing basis. Employee satisfaction surveys were initiated, and the committee made recommendations to the management team based on the feedback. This helped make sure that feedback from staff was "translated" for the management team.

Where will coaching help? Which parties?

Since the CEO was a very strong Expressive, he asked the consultants to stay on in a "coaching" capacity to him for the following year, to help his communication and style versatility skills to grow.

Epilogue of the Case Study

A year after the company retreat, a major change had occurred in the company. Communication patterns had shifted significantly, guided by regular feedback from the staff. The CEO was happy, in that he felt his message was finally getting through. He had moments when he needed to walk through the vision once more, but he combined that with other communication approaches that met the staff's need for detail. Satisfaction was strongly up, and the communication side of the surveys rated the company over 90 percent on "quality of staff communication."

— CHAPTER ELEVEN —

MODEL #8:
MOVING BEYOND THE CONFLICT

BACKGROUND OF THE MOVING BEYOND MODEL

The Moving Beyond model has been developed by the author based on the seminal work of Elisabeth Kubler-Ross in her book *On Death and Dying*.[1] This version has been modified to focus on conflict settings as opposed to situations of terminal illness, which was the focus of Kubler-Ross's work. In addition, the model has been reinforced and influenced by the work of William Bridges[2] and his process of helping people work through significant change.

The Moving Beyond model is the most psychologically focused model in the book. As the Dynamics of Trust model and attribution theory showed, it is human nature for each party to become hurt and blame the other side, erroneously attribute bad intentions to the other side, and build up or exaggerate the "wrong" done to them. This can create an enormous barrier to resolution—the inability of a party or parties to let go and move beyond the conflict. It is the "letting go" process that the Moving Beyond model addresses. We ask a

1. Elisabeth Kubler-Ross, *On Death and Dying* (New York: Scribner, 1969).
2. William Bridges, *Transitions: Making Sense of Life's Changes* (New York: Addison Wesley, 1980).

great deal of the parties when we practice conflict resolution. We ask parties to take the "hurt," the anger that they have lived with for a long time and to "get over it" in a very short period of time. In some cases, the main reason a conflict doesn't settle or resolve, even when it appears that the resolution meets everyone's interests, is that one or more parties are unable to let the conflict go, to emotionally allow it to be resolved, to reach closure.

Essentially, letting go and moving beyond is a form of grieving. The source and meaning of the word "grieve" is "to carry a heavy burden," and the process of moving beyond, of reaching an end to the grieving is to let go of that burden and put it to rest. In conflict situations it is often critical to help the parties explore what letting go of the conflict means, what accepting a resolution looks like. For this reason, Kubler-Ross's process of grieving along with Bridges's work around transitions are used as the basis for the model.

In Kubler-Ross's view, the grieving process has five steps: Denial, Anger, Bargaining, Depression, and Acceptance. Since depression is a clinical diagnosis, it wasn't directly useful or applicable in this model. Bargaining in Kubler-Ross's model is really just a form of denial revisited, and in the Moving Beyond model bargaining is included in both the Denial and Anger stages.

Complementary work done by Bridges looked at the process of change and transition, and identified three stages:

1. an Ending, followed by
2. a period of Confusion and Distress, followed by
3. a New Beginning.

In Bridges's view, people can get stuck in either of the first two steps, which will prevent them from finding the new beginning and moving forward.

From the Moving Beyond model's perspective, Kubler-Ross's and Bridges's views of reaching closure and moving on line up nicely in the following three steps:

- **Stage One: Denial**—Denial in many ways is the process of refusing to accept that something has ended, that something we don't like has happened to change our life. We ignore the problem(s), we invent reasons why it has nothing to do with us, and we vehemently deny reality in a bid to keep the status quo.
- **Stage Two: Anger**—Anger, confusion, and distress are all connected, are all a sane reaction to dealing with situations we don't want and don't like.
- **Stage Three: Acceptance**—Acceptance fits well with a New Beginning. Once we accept that we cannot simply stamp our feet and get everything we want, once we recognize that we need to find the best solution and move on, we begin to focus on a New Beginning, on life after the conflict is gone.

DIAGNOSIS WITH THE MOVING BEYOND MODEL

Based on the above, then, the Moving Beyond model identifies that in relation to conflict, there are three broad stages that people go through when dealing with difficult issues, as shown below:

The Moving Beyond Model

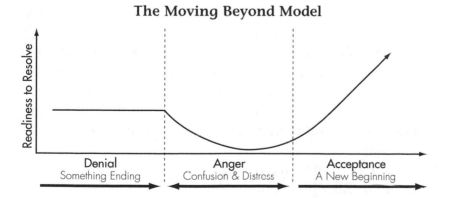

STAGE ONE: DENIAL

Denial in the field of conflict resolution typically relates to each party denying and/or refusing to accept the problem, the situation, or their role and contribution to the conflict. This links well to Bridges's idea of an ending: a relationship has ended (divorce), a business deal has gone sour (contract dispute), a person is injured in a car accident and their lifestyle is forever changed (a tort claim), a worker is fired (wrongful dismissal). In these situations, refusal to accept the situation causes each party to do one or more of the following:

- Denial of any significant contribution or responsibility for the problem;
- Denial of even being a party to the conflict or problem ("I'm not even sure why I'm here....");
- If acknowledging they did anything wrong, asserting that the other party's wrongdoing dwarfs their own and makes it irrelevant;
- Attributing all blame to the other party and ignoring or minimizing any actions or information that contradict that blame;
- Refusing to accept that this problem will or should change their life in any way, shape, or form;
- Amplifying feelings of hurt and attributing the cause solely to the other party, while denying or ignoring any information that contradicts this;
- Making offers to settle with terms that are extremely one-sided and carry a negative "attitude," which means that there is no real attempt at resolution. The "bargaining" in this case is typically intended to demonstrate how reasonable the offering party is, and how unreasonable the other party is;
- A complete and total inability to see the issues to any degree from the other parties' point of view.

From a diagnostic point of view, a party is in Denial whenever they are demonstrating some or all of the above behaviours.

STAGE TWO: ANGER

While Anger is a familiar part of conflict, what isn't clear is that that Anger only arrives once a party begins taking the conflict seriously. In Denial, we live in a world where it really isn't our problem, where the reality of the situation has not sunk in. When it dawns on us that, yes, this is my problem to deal with, that it isn't going away, and that it is going to change my life, anger quickly follows. As Kubler-Ross notes:

> If our first reaction to catastrophic news is, "No, it's not true, no, it cannot involve me," this has to give way to a new reaction, when it finally dawns on us: "Oh, yes, it is me, it was not a mistake."[3]

When it finally dawns on us that we are a part of the conflict and that we have to engage in dealing with it, that we cannot ignore it and it won't just go away, it is then that Anger sets in. This phase blends nicely with Bridges's description of this phase as one of "confusion and distress." The uncertainty and confusion causes fear, and when this is combined with seeing the other party at fault for the whole situation, Anger is the result.

Anger, of course, can be very difficult to deal with as a practitioner, mainly because anger is a wide-angle scattershot weapon, one that gets applied in many directions indiscriminately. In lawsuits it's common for each party to be angry with the other side, angry with the other side's lawyer, angry with the court system itself, angry with their own lawyer, angry with innocent third parties for not taking sides, and on and on.

Sometimes, a party will begin bargaining with the other side while still in the Anger phase, but the offers are frequently what are called "Up yours!" offers. In other words, they are

3. Kubler-Ross, p. 63.

offers intended to insult and demean the other party, and are not genuine attempts at reaching a resolution. Their goal is to vent their anger on the other party in any way they can.

From a diagnostic point of view, a party is in the Anger phase when they are venting, attacking, insulting or demeaning the other party, or, conversely, refusing to communicate or engage with them in any way. In addition, a significant feature of the Anger phase is a party's inability to hear any new information or any information they don't like. In the Anger phase, the flow of emotion is one-directional, from within the party out to anyone and anything that is perceived to be part of the problem. While little responsibility for the conflict is yet to be accepted by a party in Anger, the fact that they're angry at all indicates they are taking the issues seriously. When a party moves to the Anger phase and out of Denial, significant progress is being made.

STAGE THREE: ACCEPTANCE

The third and final stage and the stage practitioners need to help parties move toward is Acceptance. Acceptance can mean a variety of things in different situations, such as:

- Accepting that they are part of the problem and need to participate in resolving it;
- Accepting that they contributed to the problem in some way, and that they acknowledge that to the other side;
- Accepting that they want this over with and that they want to move on;
- Accepting that they will not get their way entirely, and that the solution must accommodate everyone;
- Accepting that the other side is perhaps not as "evil" as first thought;
- Accepting that the other side has a (somewhat) legitimate point of view;

- Accepting that the other side was doing their best, that they had constructive intentions (regardless of how it turned out);
- Accepting that the conflict can (and possibly should) be over, that "closure" is within reach.

In Bridges's view, the Acceptance phase is called "A New Beginning," which again links nicely to the idea of Acceptance. When a party finally accepts that a resolution can be reached, that it's time to move on, they often shift their focus away from the conflict and begin exploring what their life might be like when this conflict is over and done. They focus on a new beginning, a fresh start, and see themselves finally letting this go and getting on with their life.

From a diagnostic point of view, a party is in the Acceptance stage when they begin to negotiate in a way that actually tries to solve the problem rather than punish the other side. When a party is willing to acknowledge their behaviour was not perfect and is willing to say that to the other side, that indicates the party is in an Acceptance mode. When blame and fault become less important than getting a resolution, when arguing about "the principles" of the conflict is less important than moving on, this typically indicates the movement toward Acceptance.

One of the critical learnings from this model is to understand how parties actually move toward Acceptance and new beginnings. Most people avoid confrontation and conflict, and because of this when they hit the Anger phase, they panic and retreat from Anger back into Denial. Anger, confusion, and distress are difficult for most of us to experience for very long. Denial, on the other hand, is relatively comfortable. "Problem, what problem?" is perhaps the theme for Denial. Consequently, when a problem arises and we finally get past Denial only to run headlong into Anger, a common response is to retreat back to Denial. This creates a cycle of Denial-to-Anger then back to

Denial again, a cycle that can keep people frozen in the conflict for a long, long time.

Using the Moving Beyond model, it should be clear that when one or more parties become angry, confused, and distressed, this is actually a good thing,[4] as it means that the parties are moving in the right direction. Rather than retreat to Denial, we need to continue working through the Anger until Acceptance is reached.

CASE STUDY: MOVING BEYOND DIAGNOSIS

In the Case Study, Bob and Sally both start in the Denial phase and move through various phases through the mediation process. Diane starts in the Anger stage, where she has been stuck for a while. For each of the parties we'll identify and diagnose the phases they're in and the behaviour that leads to.

Bob:

| Denial: | Once the competition took place and the conflict started, Bob entered the Denial phase immediately, denying any possibility that Diane was actually more qualified than he was. He dealt with the issue in a rights-based way until that was no longer possible, and when he exhausted all appeals became even more entrenched in Denial. Some of the issues Bob remained in Denial about included:

• Fundamentally, Bob was in denial that the employer had the right to change job descriptions and to arrange the structure of the workplace. Bob simply could not accept that fact when the result was not in his favour.
• Bob had consistently chosen to do no customer service work and had taken no |

---

4. Within reason, of course. This is not a suggestion that rage potentially leading to violence is a "normal" part of the resolution process and needs to be accepted. Practitioners must make good judgments about the level of anger they are dealing with and act accordingly. The message here is simply that when parties get angry, it's an important sign of movement toward taking the issues seriously, and because of this toward resolution.

	customer service training. He ignored the fact he had made this choice, blaming management for this. • Bob had the competition re-run due to unfairness, but even when the union deemed it fair he refused to accept it. He was in Denial over the fact that the process itself might just have been fair and reasonable in the circumstances. • Bob denied that his failure had anything to do with himself, believing instead that management was somehow "out to get him." • Bob refused to accept that the old workplace structure had ended, and he envisioned stonewalling until things were put back to the way they had been since he was hired.
Anger:	Bob moved back and forth between Denial and Anger. Some of the areas where Bob moved into Anger included: • Bob would "mind his own business," i.e., ignore Diane (refuse to accept her promotion), but as soon as she followed up with him he lost his temper and lashed out at her. • Bob would hang around with a few other staff members who disliked Sally and her proposed changes, and the more they talked, the angrier the group got. This would recede into Denial when they all went back to work, waiting for another trigger to move again into Anger.

(Continued)

| | • Bob's uncooperative approach spoke of a deep Anger, albeit passive-aggressive, one that he was willing to risk his job over.
• Bob displayed both confusion and distress, frequently getting his facts or dates wrong when trying to make a point. |
| **Acceptance:** | This will be left for the "Strategic" part of the model. |

Sally:

| **Denial:** | Sally had a difficult mandate—to make changes to long-standing workplace structures with a strong union presence and a long set of traditions. In going about this, Sally was in Denial about a few key points:

• Sally didn't want to recognize the scope of the changes being asked of the staff—she kept saying, "What's the problem? These changes aren't so bad."
• Sally denied that her approach was in any way part of the problem. In reality, she was quite autocratic about the nature of the changes to Bob and Diane's roles, and refused to consider any other options. She did this while maintaining that she was flexible and open to feedback.
• She kept telling Diane that Bob would come around, just keep trying to be nice to him.
• Sally didn't recognize that for the staff, an era, in a sense, had ended. They had done |

	things the same way for a very long time, and now a new way of managing the department was here. She refused to recognize the significance of the changes being made.
Anger:	Sally displayed little Anger overtly, although she talked a lot about her "frustration" with Bob, and this frustration was evident in her behaviour. • She would avoid Bob on many days when she felt that she was too frustrated to be constructive with him. • Since she didn't see the changes as all that onerous, she was confused as to why not only Bob, but other staff, were so hostile to what she was trying to implement. • She would send curt, pointed emails to Bob directing him back to Diane. Bob read these emails as quite angry in tone.
Acceptance:	This will be left for the "Strategic" part of the model.

Diane:

Denial:	Diane was in very little Denial in this case, and had moved directly to Anger. In general, she saw how angry Bob was and was equally frustrated with Sally, whom she saw as giving her an impossible task—to give Bob direction when Bob simply refused to work with her as his supervisor. Diane, of the three, saw the situation most clearly.

Anger:	Diane was deeply stuck in the Anger stage. She was: • Angry with Bob for refusing to recognize her new position and for disrespecting and humiliating her in the workplace with his flat-out refusal to listen to her, along with his tendency to completely ignore Diane's presence for days at a time. • Angry and confused about why Sally was allowing this to go on, and for implying that if Diane were "nice" enough to Bob he'd get over it and start to listen to her. In addition, she was angry with Sally for not supporting her when she asked that Bob be disciplined.
Acceptance:	This will be left for the "Strategic" part of the model.

As you can see, the three parties were stuck at various places in the first two stages of the Moving Beyond model. There had been some "negotiating" between Sally and Bob during the process, but it was "false" bargaining. The offers from each were so one-sided that they inflamed the situation rather than resolved it. For example, Bob suggested that Sally treat him as if he actually were an AS-1 and keep everything else the same, and they'd worry about the actual classification later. This offer by Bob was completely unacceptable in that it missed the whole point of the changes. In other words, it wasn't a legitimate attempt to resolve the situation; it was a form of Denial on Bob's part. For Sally's part, she suggested that Bob give in and accept everything, and she'd promise that no discipline would occur. This offer was nothing short of demanding capitulation, something completely unacceptable to Bob and indicating that Sally was still negotiating from a position of Denial and/or Anger. That kind of bargaining or negotiation will typically further entrench the parties rather than move them toward resolution.

Let's take a look now at how the Moving Beyond model guides the practitioner toward strategic choices based on the diagnosis above.

STRATEGIC DIRECTION FROM THE MOVING BEYOND MODEL

Strategically, the Moving Beyond model gives very broad direction that relies heavily on basic conflict resolution "microskills." The value of the strategic direction the model offers is that it helps practitioners use the appropriate skills at the right time. There are two key points strategically-speaking.

- **Strategy #1—Help Parties Move Step-by-Step Toward Acceptance:** Each party must move through the process roughly in order, from Denial, through Anger, and only then to Acceptance. Trying to skip a stage or ignore a stage will simply cause the party to stay stuck in that stage. If someone is in Denial, trying to go straight on to Acceptance rarely helps the party actually let go of the conflict and move on. If someone is deeply angry, attempting to suppress this anger or suggesting, "anger won't help you" may get nicer behaviour on the surface (at best), but will not help the party truly move out of Anger and start moving beyond the conflict. Staying stuck in Denial or Anger will tend to produce "false" bargaining and little movement toward actual resolution.

- **Strategy #2:** Each step of Denial, Anger, and Acceptance in the Model requires the application of different skills and interventions; each step needs to be treated differently. The figure below outlines the different skills and interventions that apply at each step.

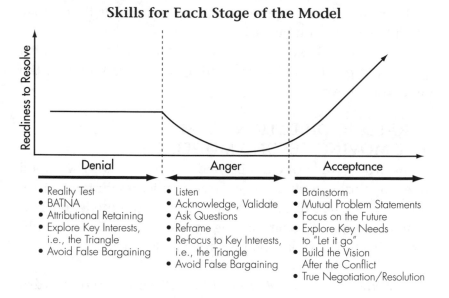

Skills for Each Stage of the Model

Denial	Anger	Acceptance
• Reality Test • BATNA • Attributional Retaining • Explore Key Interests, i.e., the Triangle • Avoid False Bargaining	• Listen • Acknowledge, Validate • Ask Questions • Reframe • Re-focus to Key Interests, i.e., the Triangle • Avoid False Bargaining	• Brainstorm • Mutual Problem Statements • Focus on the Future • Explore Key Needs to "Let it go" • Build the Vision After the Conflict • True Negotiation/Resolution

Denial: Strategies for Managing the Denial Stage

The first step is to help get the party out of Denial.[5] The practitioner needs to focus on the following skills and interventions to accomplish this:

1. **Explore Key Interests:** The foundation of many skills is exploring and probing to learn the party's key interests, their wants, needs, fears, concerns, hopes, etc. Learning these and understanding what areas the party is in Denial about sets the stage for the reality testing to follow. For example, if the party says they want this conflict resolved yet refuses to engage in any problem solving behaviour, this contradiction can be used to reality-test the party later.

5. It should be noted that when dealing with Denial, it is not the practitioner's job to force someone out of their Denial, as people sometimes stay in Denial because they simply cannot handle the Anger or the level of change needed. As practitioners, we should help them explore the stage of Denial, help them look at Acceptance and what it would take. Ultimately, it must be up to the parties themselves if they want to let go and move beyond the conflict.

2. **Reality Test, BATNA,[6] Attributional Retraining[7]**: Reality testing is the generic term for a number of related approaches, including BATNA exploration and attributional retraining. All of these skills help us gather information about the situation and the party's key interests, then gently exposes contradictory behaviour, data conflicts, and outcomes that are not desirable if the party continues on their current path. In the case of attributional retraining, it challenges the attributions the party is making, many of which are skewed or incorrect having been arrived at through a self-serving bias. While there is a wide range of named skills and interventions to choose from in the "reality testing" arena, the net result has to be challenging the party's assumptions and choices with the goal of helping them assess the situation they're in more clearly. By helping them look where they don't want to look, by gently bringing into focus the parts of the situation that are difficult, the party starts to move out of Denial. Be aware that the next step when this is accomplished is typically Anger.

3. **Avoid False Bargaining:** There is a tendency for some parties to want to bargain or negotiate while still stuck in Denial. Generally speaking, offers made during the Denial phase are at best one-sided and at worst convince the other party that there is no chance of a resolution. Since offers made during the Denial stage are not reflective of any real assessment of the situation, they have the potential to inflame the other party further. When one party, who has yet to recognize they have some contribution or liability in a situation, makes an offer that amounts to "nuisance value," it can provoke the other party to walk out in order to show them how serious they are. This approach helps no one.

Note that in a very few situations agreements can be reached with people in Denial, but only if the desire to remain in

---

6. BATNA is an acronym for Best Alternative To a Negotiated Agreement. This is one of the principles of Interest-Based Negotiation from Roger Fisher and Bill Ury at the Harvard Project on Negotiation.
7. This is a specific approach to reality testing from the Dynamics of Trust model.

Denial is strong enough to bring some concessions. The net effect, though, is to allow the party to remain in Denial about the main issues for the near future, which may mean that the resolution will not last. For example, suppose that in a family business setting the father (and CEO) is in Denial that his daughter is not interested in running the family business and wants to leave. The father, in Denial about what his daughter really wants in her life, will offer a large raise to keep her in the company. The daughter reluctantly agrees. This strategy may work in the short term in that the daughter agrees to stay, but may be staying for the wrong reasons (she, too, is in Denial about how guilty she feels leaving, so she decides to stay for one more year, with the rationale of saving her money to fund what she really wants to do). The father, in reaching this resolution, stays in Denial about the core issue (his daughter's desire to leave) at least for another year.

The goal in dealing with Denial, essentially, is to help the party move past and out of Denial. Next stop, Anger.

Anger: Strategies for Managing the Anger Stage

When a party is in the Anger stage, the process must be handled carefully. Anger is not a problem to be solved, nor something to be ignored or suppressed. Taking a "Just the facts, Ma'am" approach will do little to help the party move forward. Anger is an emotion that needs to be worked through and processed as respectfully as possible. The practitioner should focus on the following:

1. **Listen:** Actively listening to someone who is angry is one of the most effective ways to defuse the anger. Many times, the need to be heard is underlying a great deal of Anger. Allow and encourage venting, within reason.

2. **Focus on the Emotional Interests by Acknowledging and Validating**[8]**:** Feelings are legitimate, even if the reasoning behind them might not be. Acknowledge and validate the feelings, without pronouncing the party "right" on the issues. Take the feelings seriously, and reserve the reality testing and the problem solving for the Denial and Acceptance stages.

3. **Ask Questions:** Asking a good question indicates respect and concern, both of which are in short supply to the angry person.

4. **Reframe:** Anger brings out the most extreme thoughts and feelings. Reframing retains the important interest and objective of the angry party while literally "reframing" the issue in a way that helps move it toward problem solving.

5. **Refocus to Key Interests:** As the Anger starts to subside, start to refocus the party onto his or her important interests.

6. **Avoid False Bargaining:** When angry, parties sometimes throw out offers to resolve the conflict, but offers made out of frustration will tend to insult or demean the other party. Offers to settle made in Anger tend to be more an expression of the Anger rather than a genuine offer to settle. Focus back on the feelings, and defer settlement discussions to the Acceptance stage.

One of the worst steps to take in the Anger phase is to attempt reality testing or problem solving. No matter how effectively done, it will almost always inflame the Anger more and polarize the parties further. Anger must be processed and moved through; Acceptance is the stage where most resolutions will take place.

---

8. See the Triangle of Satisfaction model for an in-depth look at strategies for the different types of interests, specifically Emotional/Psychological interests.

Acceptance: Strategies for Managing the Acceptance Stage

When a party hits the Acceptance stage, they not only are ready to let this conflict go and move on, they are often eager to. This doesn't mean the party won't negotiate hard or hold out until their important interests are met, but it does mean that they are ready to negotiate in good faith, listen to what the other party wants without as much anger, and stay focused on reaching a resolution. In the Acceptance stage, all the skills surrounding effective problem solving apply, including:

1. **Focus on Key Substantive and Process Interests**[9]: This is the stage where the result, along with the process, is important. Keep a strong focus on the parties' interests, especially the substantive and procedural ones. The emotional interests were (hopefully) addressed to a great degree in the Anger stage.

2. **Brainstorming:** Brainstorming is a key tool for effective problem solving, and should be used liberally.

3. **Mutual Problem Statements:** Mutual Problem Statements are a type of brainstorming that can help the parties develop solutions that have a reasonable chance of working for both parties.

4. **Build the "Post-Conflict" Vision:** Good conflict resolution focuses the parties on the future, and the Acceptance stage is where this will be effective. Trying to bring a future focus in the Anger stage, for example, paints the picture of the person being angry for a long time to come, which obviously won't help with resolution. In the Acceptance stage, help the parties think about what their world will look and feel like when this conflict over. This creates a positive motivation for resolution.

9. See the Triangle of Satisfaction model for an in-depth look at strategies for the different types of interests.

5. **Explore Key Needs to "Let It Go":** Key questions, such as "What will you need to let this whole situation go and move on?" can be very powerful when asked in the Acceptance stage.

6. **True Negotiation and Resolution:** Negotiations in the Acceptance stage will be focused on actually resolving the problems, unlike in the previous two stages. In this stage, parties will listen to and hear what the other party needs and will try to meet some of that. Any consideration of what the other party needs would be out of the question in either of the other two stages.

Once parties arrive at the Acceptance stage, this doesn't mean they'll stay there forever. Many things can happen that may throw them back into Anger or even Denial, and the practitioner must use the skills listed to work with each party at whatever stage they move into. By applying the appropriate skills in each of the stages, the practitioner keeps the parties moving through the model in the overall direction of Acceptance.

CASE STUDY: STRATEGIC DIRECTION WITH THE MOVING BEYOND MODEL

Strategically, the Moving Beyond model can be very helpful in understanding how parties move from being stuck in Denial or Anger to reaching some level of Acceptance and resolution. In our Case Study, for example, trying to argue with Bob or force Bob to change while he remained in Denial and/or Anger (as Sally had been doing) simply didn't work. It reinforced and strengthened the level of Denial. Similarly, when dealing with Bob or Sally's Anger through argument and accusation, the parties get defensive and stuck in a Denial-to-Anger cycle that never reaches or approaches Acceptance.

Some ideas for applying the Moving Beyond model to our Case Study follow below.

Bob: Dealing with Denial
Explore Key Interests:

- A number of Bob's key interests have already surfaced, including:
    - The promotion, either this one or another one;
    - To be included in the communications loop;
    - To have access to and contact with his manager, Sally;
    - To have a workplace he enjoys coming into;
    - To feel that he is respected for his years of service, and to feel that he is being treated fairly.

Reality Test to Move Past Denial:
- Bob is stuck in the past, in wanting a department structure that apparently will not continue to exist. The workplace is changing. Some reality testing questions that could begin to move Bob past the Denial might be:
    - What are the reasons you tend to choose more technical roles rather than customer service roles? What would happen if you were offered customer service roles in the future?
    - What are management's rights in terms of structuring the workplace and assigning work to staff?
    - What does the union say about this? Does the union say that management is within their rights in this process?
    - How long will management accept the struggle between you, Diane, and Sally? What might management do if the current relationships continue to be disruptive?
    - How likely is it that continuing to be difficult will get you what you want?

- If there were a better way to address these problems, how interested would you be in trying it?
- If Sally were really trying to get rid of you, why hasn't she fired you or disciplined you in the last few months, when even the union appears to agree with her?
- Bob, if management has the right to structure the workplace the way they want, and if they used a fair process (at least one that your union says is fair), and if they have no intention of structuring it the way that you really want, what do you, as an employee here, need to do?

Bob, when asked a number of these questions above, will have a hard time remaining in Denial as he reflects on the issues these questions raise. At some point the reality and focus of the questions will get Bob out of Denial, typically opening up the feelings and emotions he's been going through in this situation.

Bob: Dealing with Anger
Listen, Acknowledge the Anger:
Bob felt demeaned, taken for granted, and not recognized for the good work he had done. He felt that Diane's promotion meant he was no good, that Sally didn't value him at all. He couldn't live with these feelings. The practitioner should listen, acknowledge,[10] and reframe this, which will help Bob process and reduce the anger without driving him back into Denial:

- You've felt unappreciated, taken for granted, not listened to, is that it?
- You've put a lot of effort into your role here, and you don't think Sally sees this.

(Continued)

10. Face-to-face skills such as Active Listening rarely translate well on the page. The acknowledgements listed are just indications of the direction taken, not a representation of the best wording or style for these skills.

- You want Sally to let you know she does value your contribution here, right?
- It sounds like the workplace is pretty unpleasant right now, and you'd like that to change.

Working through the Anger stage can take a few minutes, a few hours, even days, depending on a number of factors, including the depth of the relationships the conflict relates to, the importance to the parties, the attributions being made, and many more. Bob needed help to work through his emotions without being asked for a solution.

Bob: Moving into Acceptance
Focusing on Interests, Moving to Acceptance and Beyond:
Once the Anger has been vented, once Bob feels he is being listened to, he may be ready to consider what he needs to move beyond the conflict, what he needs to reach some degree of Acceptance. The following questions will focus Bob on his interests,[11] on what he wants, given that he now knows the status quo is not an option:

- You've said that you need to accept that management is implementing these changes. What do you need so you'd be ready to work constructively with Sally and Diane to make this change work?
- What would you need from Sally so you knew that she valued your work and contribution, while at the same time Sally knew that you would accept the new structure?
- What would you and Diane need to agree upon so that you'd take direction from her willingly?
- What would need to happen so you'd look forward to coming in to work again?

11. At this point, refer to the Triangle of Satisfaction model for an in-depth look at how to most effectively access and use the three different types of interests Bob has: the Result Bob is looking for, the Process to best get there, and what Bob needs to feel good about accepting a resolution.

- How would you respond to Sally giving you constructive feedback, to prepare you for the next promotion competition? What would you say if she were prepared to help you?

By applying different approaches at each stage, the practitioner can help Bob get out of Denial, process the Anger, and move toward constructive solutions and Acceptance.

Sally: Dealing with Denial
Reality Test to Move Past Denial:

- The main areas of Sally's Denial are around the magnitude of the changes, and the autocratic nature of her process. The following questions might help get Sally out of Denial:
  - How much input have staff had into the changes you've been making? (*Well, none, they've been imposed from Headquarters.*)
  - How is the staff in general reacting to the changes being imposed on them? (*Not very well, but they should just accept them.*)
  - What kinds of things have you been doing, directly, to help them accept changes they really don't like? (*Well, I haven't had time to hold their hand, I guess.*)
  - How successful have you been just expecting or demanding them to like and accept the changes? (*It hasn't been successful at all.*)
  - As the manager who is responsible for getting the team what they need to move forward? (*I am, but.....*)
  - How happy has Diane been with being told to "be nice" to Bob? (*She's not very happy.*) How effective has it been? (*It hasn't, I guess*)

(Continued)

- Who will be held accountable for effectively implementing these changes? (*At the end of the day, I will.*)

With these reality testing questions, Sally starts to see that at
the end of the day, she has to make this work. This brings out
the frustration she's been feeling.

Sally: Dealing with Anger
Listen, Acknowledge the Anger:
Sally felt like she was being targeted and attacked for decisions made elsewhere, when she had expected that her
staff would support her. She was angry and frustrated, and
felt like many of the staff, led by Bob, were hanging her out
to dry. The practitioner should listen, acknowledge,[12] and
reframe this, which will reduce the anger without driving
Sally back into Denial:

- You've felt attacked and blamed for the changes here…
- You've put a lot of effort into trying to make these
changes as painless as possible for the staff, and you
don't think Bob sees this.
- You want Bob to let you know that he'll listen to and
respect your decisions, right?
- It sounds like the workplace is pretty unpleasant right
now, and you'd like that to change. Is that right?

Sally: Moving into Acceptance
Focusing on Interests, Moving to Acceptance and Beyond:
Once the anger has been vented, once Sally feels she is
being listened to, she may be ready to consider what she
needs to do to resolve the conflict, what she needs to reach

---

12. Face-to-face skills such as Active Listening rarely translate well on the page. The acknowledgements listed are just indications of the direction taken, not a representation of the best wording or
style for these skills.

some degree of Acceptance. The following questions focus Sally on her interests[13]:

- You've recognized that the process has been autocratic; what might you do to change that with Bob?
- What kind of feedback and input could you consider from Bob so he sees that you're willing to work with some of his concerns?
- What kind of flexibility do you have in relation to Bob's role, if that helps get Bob's buy-in to these changes?

By applying different approaches at each stage, the practitioner can help Sally recognize some of the issues she'd been ignoring (Denial), process the Anger, and move toward constructive solutions and Acceptance.

Diane: Dealing with Anger

Diane, you will recall, is not in a lot of Denial; she's stuck in the Anger stage, feeling helpless and unable to solve the problem. We'll move right to the Anger stage with Diane.

Listen, Acknowledge the Anger:

Diane felt caught in the middle, told to work with Bob and "be nice," while not being given any authority to deal with the situation. She didn't feel she got any help or support from Sally, and felt badly treated by Bob. The practitioner should listen, acknowledge,[14] and reframe this, which will help reduce the anger and facilitate moving the focus to Acceptance:

- You've felt helpless to fix this, and caught in between Bob and Sally...
- You've put a lot of effort into trying to make these changes work with Bob, but he won't listen to you, right?

(Continued)

---

13. At this point, refer to the Triangle of Satisfaction model for an in-depth look at how to most effectively access and use three different types of interests Sally has: the Result Sally is looking for, the Process to best get there, and what Sally needs to feel good about accepting a resolution.

14. Face-to-face skills such as Active Listening rarely translate well on the page. The acknowledgements listed are just indications of the direction taken, not a representation of the best wording or style for these skills.

- You want Bob to willingly accept that he takes direction from you.
- It sounds like the workplace is pretty unpleasant right now and you'd like that to change. Is that right?
- What impact has losing your temper with Bob had on the situation?

Diane: Moving into Acceptance
Focusing on Interests, Moving to Acceptance and Beyond: Once the anger has been vented, once Diane feels she is being listened to, she may be ready to just focus on supporting whatever solutions Bob and Sally come up with. The following questions focus Diane on her interests[15]:

- If Bob starts to work constructively, what else would you need so you feel that the situation is really improving?
- What support do you need from Sally to do your job?
- What do you need to hear from Bob to let the past go?
- What do you think Bob needs to hear from you about how you'll handle stressful situations with him in the future?
- What do you think you can do to put an end to the harassment complaint?

By helping Diane work through her Anger, and by focusing her forward to the Acceptance stage, there is a good chance the past can be left behind in favour of a better future.

ASSESSING AND APPLYING THE MOVING BEYOND MODEL

From a diagnostic point of view, the Moving Beyond model is fairly high-level, identifying a broad pattern people go through in trying to move past a conflict and let it go. It allows

15. At this point, refer to the Triangle of Satisfaction model for an in-depth look at how to most effectively access and use three different types of interests Diane has: the Result Diane is looking for, the Process to best get there, and what Diane needs to feel good about accepting a resolution.

practitioners to identify and see exactly where people get "stuck" in a conflict, becoming unable to let it go or resolve it. By helping practitioners assess this, it rates high on the diagnostic scale.

From a strategic point of view the model is more general, relying on well-tested and well-established communication skills to help parties move through the stages. That said, the stages themselves serve as an invaluable road map for the practitioner to identify the barriers to settlement, and to then apply the appropriate skills in the right stage to help the parties let go of the conflict and move beyond. For this reason it rates medium-high on the strategic scale.

PRACTITIONER'S WORKSHEET FOR THE MOVING BEYOND MODEL

Denial:

What are the parties in Denial about? Where are they stuck? • *Party A:* • *Party B:* What are the Parties' Key Interests? • *Party A:* • *Party B:*	 Reality Testing Questions for Party A: Reality Testing Questions for Party B:

Anger to Acceptance:

What does each party not feel heard about? What do they need listened to and acknowledged to help them through Anger to Acceptance?

Party A:

Party B:

ADDITIONAL CASE STUDY—CIRCLE OF CONFLICT

The Workplace Assault Case

An employee, Sheila, worked at a senior citizens home for about two years, and was terminated for an incident involving another employee, Helen. Sheila and Helen took an immediate dislike to each other and coped with it by simply ignoring each other. A new supervisor took over the area, and the supervisor and Helen became close friends. Over the past year, Helen and Sheila started to have frequent clashes in the workplace. The supervisor simply told both of them to behave.

One day, Sheila came in to work late. The supervisor listened to Sheila's explanation of problems in her personal life (her husband had moved out on the weekend, leaving her alone with their child) but still gave her a written warning about being late. This upset Sheila. Later that day in the staff room Helen apparently taunted Sheila with the discipline and the problems she was having at home. Sheila became enraged and attacked Helen, squeezing her throat until she couldn't breathe. Co-workers pulled Sheila off Helen. Sheila was sent home, and fired the next day. No discipline was given to Helen. Sheila sued the employer for wrongful dismissal.

At mediation, Sheila downplayed the attack and claimed that the three witnesses were Helen's friends, and talked a great deal about Helen receiving no discipline for instigating the fight. The employer ignored the lack of progressive discipline in the case, and downplayed the supervisor not addressing past incidents between Sheila and Helen, focusing on the company's written policy that any acts of a physical nature would result in immediate termination.

In caucus, Sheila was demanding $50,000 even though her own lawyer kept telling her the most she could get was two to three months' salary, a total of $10,000—and that would happen only if they won, which was not likely. Sheila would not listen.

In caucus, the employer was refusing to pay anything, stating that their policy absolved them of any liability. Their lawyer told them they definitely had risk, but the employer refused to pay any money to an employee who engaged in physical violence.

MOVING BEYOND MODEL DIAGNOSIS AND WORKSHEET: THE WORKPLACE ASSAULT CASE

Denial:

What are the parties in Denial about? Where are they stuck?

- *Sheila is in complete Denial that physically attacking someone is never acceptable.*
- *Sheila is in Denial about what her claim is worth, and the risks associated with it.*

(Continued)

- *The Employer is in Denial that their whole policy could be found flawed, setting a very poor precedent.*
- *The Employer is in Denial that their supervisor did little to address the problem early, opening them up to additional risk.*

What are their Key Interests?

Sheila:
- *To feel fairly treated.*
- *To have it acknowledged that she didn't start this fight.*
- *To get some money to pay her rent for a few months, while she looks for a job.*
- *To have some kind of reference so she could get another job.*

Employer:
- *To have their Zero Tolerance policy on violence respected.*
- *To not bring this employee back.*
- *To pay as little money as possible.*

Anger To Acceptance:

What does each party not feel heard about? What do they need listened to and acknowledged?

Sheila:
- *She didn't start the incident.*
- *Helen was trying to get her in trouble.*
- *Helen didn't receive any discipline.*
- *She is now a single parent, and needs to keep a roof over her and her child's head—she needs money.*
- *She needs some help getting a new job.*

Employer:
- *This policy is legitimate and needs to be enforced.*
- *They will not tolerate violence for any reason.*

MOVING BEYOND MODEL STRATEGIC DIRECTION: THE WORKPLACE ASSAULT CASE

Based on the diagnosis and identification of the areas of Denial and Anger, the practitioner focused on moving them out of Denial using some of the reality testing questions below:

Reality Testing Questions for Sheila:
- In our society, under what conditions is violence of any kind permitted?
- Why does the employer have this policy in the first place?
- If you went to court and won, how much do you think you'd win?
- If you went to court and lost, how much money do you think you'd owe them?
- If you need some financial help now, how many years are you prepared to wait for a court decision?
- How clear are you on how a court might calculate your damages, assuming you win?

Reality Testing Questions for the Employer:
- Given that these two had issues for a long time, how effectively did your supervisor handle this?
- How does the fact that the supervisor and Helen are close friends affect this situation?
- If Helen was indeed instigating this, what, as an employer, are your responsibilities?

(Continued)

> • How does your Zero Tolerance policy fit with past court decisions? What would happen if the court didn't uphold your policy?

After reality testing to get them out of Denial, the practitioner used listening, acknowledging, and further questioning to address and help them process their Anger. Once both parties were heading for Acceptance, good problem solving skills, detailed below, helped them come to a resolution.

Epilogue of the Case Study

Initially, Sheila's only offer to settle was $50,000, and the employer countered with zero.

After the mediator caucused and reality tested along the lines of the analysis, Sheila finally began to move out of Denial and understand that even though she was provoked, she shouldn't have attacked Helen. She also got past her Anger at the company and focused on her immediate need for money, and to get any help that the employer would offer to help her get a new job. She revised her offer to three months' salary, about $9000.

The mediator reality tested the employer, and after working through the Denial that they owed Sheila anything, and the Anger that this incident took place at all, the employer accepted that if Helen had provoked the fight they needed to address that. Because they didn't investigate the incident properly, their dismissal might not be upheld in court. They refused to consider reinstatement, but revised their offer from zero to $4500 (1.5 months' salary), plus a letter of reference, which they offered to write because Sheila was an excellent worker other than this incident. Sheila asked for two months ($6000) and the letter, and they settled on $5500, plus the letter. Both parties left feeling that this was a very unfortunate incident, but were prepared to move on.

— CHAPTER TWELVE —

CONCLUSION

This book has presented models for practitioner use in diagnosing and assessing conflict. It has presented them on the
basis that practitioners of all types—mediators, negotiators
and facilitators—will benefit greatly from learning and applying a range of conflict analysis models in their work.

But many practitioners are skilled and effective at conflict
management by just working intuitively, by doing what seems to
make sense, often with good results. So why bother learning and
developing models for conflict analysis in your practice?

The reason is simply this: working with models like these lead
the practitioner from a level of competence to a level of mastery.
As we look more broadly at growing and developing in the field
of conflict resolution, these models are essential for conflict practitioners if they wish to become more than simply competent
in their work. The path from "journeyman" to "artist" in the field
of conflict resolution is well described by Michael Lang and
Alison Taylor in their recent book, *The Making of a Mediator*.[1]
In this book, the authors define "journeyman" practitioners as

---

1. Michael Lang and Alison Taylor, *The Making of a Mediator*, (New York: Jossey-Bass, 2000).

competent, but rarely reaching the status of exceptional. For Lang and Taylor, we all strive toward exceptional skill in the field, a level of work they define as "artistry".

One reason practitioners rarely become exceptional, according to Lang and Taylor, is that journeymen mediators believe that the path to becoming an artist is to learn more and more skills, constantly adding more communication tools such as reframing, active listening, and the like to their toolbox. What is lacking for journeymen are not more skills, but rather the art of self-reflection, the ability to diagnose a conflict, intervene based on that diagnosis, and then learn from the outcome of that intervention. Without this ability for self-reflection, which begins with the ability to consciously diagnose the situation, the journeyman practitioner will not be able to advance past basic competence in the field.

> Mediators may seek to fill tool their toolboxes, believing that competency in the use of many tools is the way to achieve effective practice. Although proficiency in the use of a wide array of tools is one of the essential elements of professional practice, the mediator who does not understand the situations in which such tools are most useful will inevitably be a tinkerer—trying out a succession of tools, unaware of the reasons for using them, and unaware of why those tools have either achieved a desired result or failed to assist the parties.[2]

The Conflict Resolution Toolbox is intended as a guide for practitioners to learn, apply, test and practice with models that lead the reflective practitioner toward ever greater levels of competence and through to true artistry.

This book, therefore, urges practitioners to take these models, use them, work with them, adapt them and modify them if

2. Ibid, p. 135

necessary, and make them a core part of their conflict diagnosis and intervention practice. By doing so, we can all become reflective practitioners, and as reflective practitioners, we will continue to consolidate and build the conflict resolution field as an important profession in human society.

INDEX

Note: (cs) after a page number indicates references to case studies not otherwise identified